More [illegible]

By the Editors at Nikoli Publishing

WORKMAN PUBLISHING
NEW YORK

Library of Congress Cataloging-in-Publication Data is available.

ISBN-13: 978-0-7611-4397-0
ISBN-10: 0-7611-4397-1

Workman Publishing Company, Inc.
708 Broadway
New York, NY 10003-9555
www.workman.com

Design by Paul Gamarello and Vanessa Ray

Printed in the United States of America
First printing: April 2006

10 9 8 7 6 5 4 3 2 1

Contents

Introduction v

What is Sudoku? v

The History of Sudoku v

The Rules of Sudoku vi

Getting Started vi

Why Handmade? xi

Why Nikoli? xiii

Puzzles 1

PART 1: Easy 1

PART 2: Medium 52

PART 3: Hard 163

PART 4: Very Hard 274

Puzzle Solutions 325

Make Your Own Sudoku 407

Introduction

What is Sudoku?

A deceptively simple exercise in logic, Sudoku is a grid-based number game. Each puzzle is made up of 81 squares (called cells), which form 9 columns, 9 rows, and 9 boxes—each of which is a 3 x 3 square that is set off by a bold line.

1	2	3	4	5	6	7	8	9
4	5	6						
7	8	9						
2								
5								
8								
3								
6								
9								

The History of Sudoku

The editors of Nikoli, the leading puzzle company in Japan, discovered a puzzle called "Number Place" in an American magazine in the 1970s, and then introduced it to Japanese readers in 1984. (That puzzle was a variation on Latin Squares, developed in the eighteenth century by the Swiss mathematician Leonhard Euler, who himself had been inspired by an older puzzle called Magic Squares, which in turn can be traced to Lo Shu, an ancient Chinese puzzle.) At first the editors called the puzzle "Suuji wa dokushin ni kagiru," which means "it is best for the number to be single." That title was not only too long but also confusing, so they abbreviated it to "Sudoku"—*su* meaning number, *doku* meaning single. The name "Sudoku" is trademarked by Nikoli in Japan, so other companies are restricted to calling their puzzles "Number Place."

Sudoku did not catch on at first, but then, in 1986, the editors introduced two new rules. First, they determined that all the numbers must be arranged in a symmetrical pattern, and second, no more than thirty numbers can be revealed at the start of any puzzle. The result was magical, and Sudoku became a huge hit. In recent years, the puzzle has spread from Japan to other countries, but most of these newer puzzles are generated by computer and lack the simple beauty of the Nikoli puzzles. But more on that later.

The Rules of Sudoku

Very simple to learn, Sudoku involves no math and no calculations, but yet provides a surprisingly wide variety of logic situations. Here are the basics:

1. Place a number (1 through 9) in each blank cell.
2. Each row, column, and 3 x 3 box must contain the numbers 1 through 9 without repeating any numbers.

Getting Started

The level of difficulty depends upon how many numbers are initially revealed, which also affects the technique you should use in approaching each puzzle. But the logic is always based on the narrowing of possibilities.

Basic Pattern 1

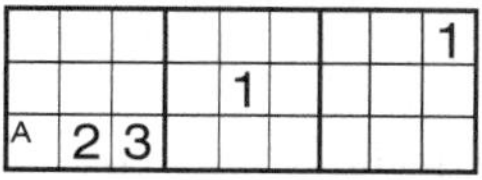

Start at the box on the left. The top two rows cannot contain the number 1 because of the 1s in the middle and right boxes. Therefore, the only place for a 1 in the first box is cell A.

Basic Pattern 2

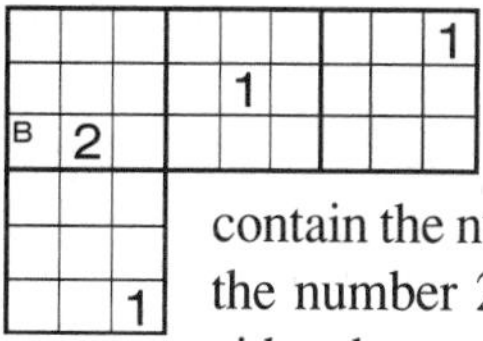

Basic Pattern 2 is similar to Pattern 1. In the upper left box, the top two rows cannot contain the number 1. The cell to the right of the number 2 cannot contain the number 1 either because of the 1 in column three in the box below. Therefore, a 1 must be placed in cell B.

Basic Pattern 3

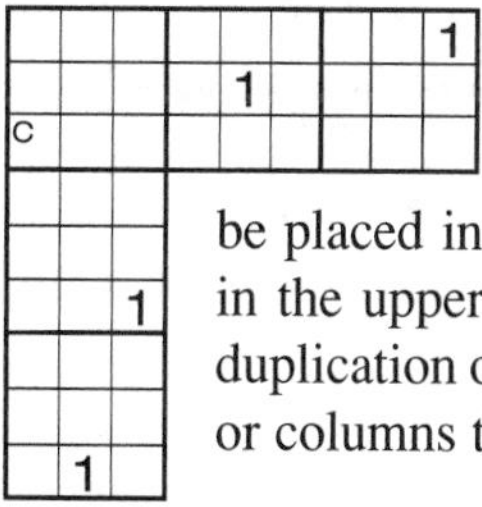

After learning Basic Patterns 1 and 2, it is easy to determine that the number 1 must be placed in cell C since it is the only cell in the upper left box that will not cause a duplication of 1s in either rows one and two or columns three and four.

Basic Pattern 4

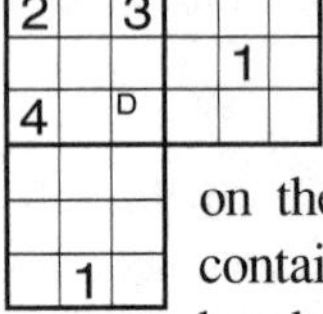

In this pattern, the middle row in the upper left box cannot contain the number 1 because of the 1 in the box on the right. And the middle column can't contain the number 1 because of the 1 in the box below. A 1 must be placed in cell D.

Basic Pattern 5

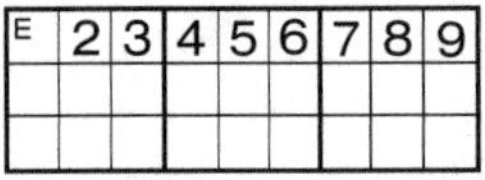

This pattern is an extremely easy one. On the top row, E is the only cell remaining in which one can place the number 1.

Advanced Pattern 1

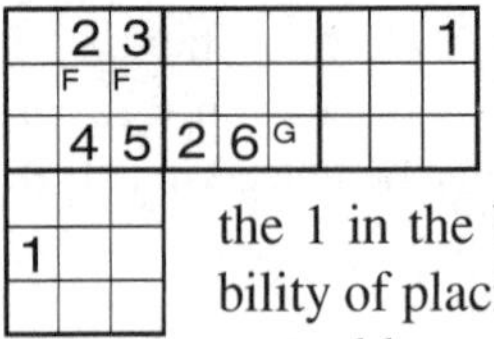

In the upper left box, the number 1 will be placed in either of the F cells because the 1 in the bottom box negates the possibility of placing 1 in the first column. In the second box, the top row cannot contain the number 1 because a 1 already appears in the top row (in the far right box). Also, the middle row cannot contain a 1 because either of the F cells will contain the number 1. Therefore, in the second box, the number 1 can only be placed in cell G.

Advanced Pattern 2

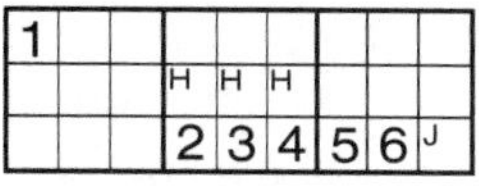

To determine where the number 1 should go in the far right box, first look at the far left box. Because of the number 1 already in the top row of the box, a 1 cannot be placed in the entire top row. In the middle box, with the cells in the bottom row already filled with the numbers 2, 3, and 4, there is no other place for the number 1 than in one of the H cells in the middle row. Therefore, with a 1 in the top row, and the necessity of a 1 in one of the H cells, the only remaining option in the far right box is to place the number 1 in cell J.

Advanced Pattern 3

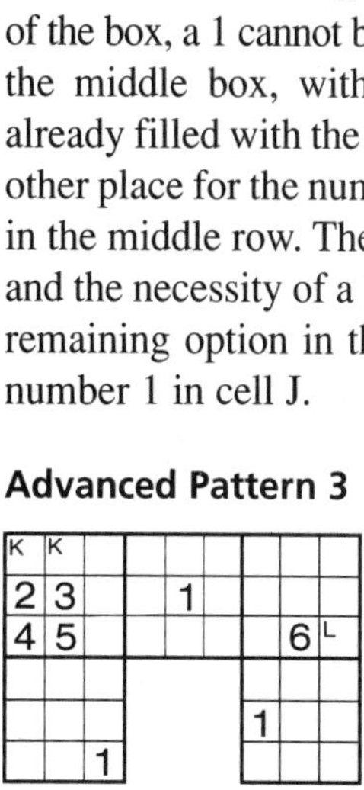

In the upper left box, the number 1 should be placed in either of the K cells. (Now no other cells in the top row may contain the number 1.) In the upper right box, the top and middle rows cannot contain a 1; its far left column cannot contain a 1 because of the cell that contains a 1 in the box below. Therefore, the number 1 must be placed in cell L.

Advanced Pattern 4

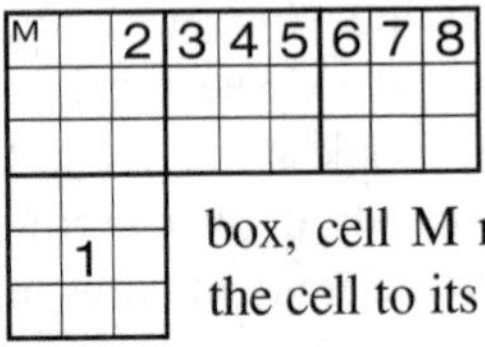

Numbers 1 and 9 are missing from the top row. Because of the 1 already in the lower left box, cell M must contain the number 1 and the cell to its right will contain the number 9.

Advanced Pattern 5

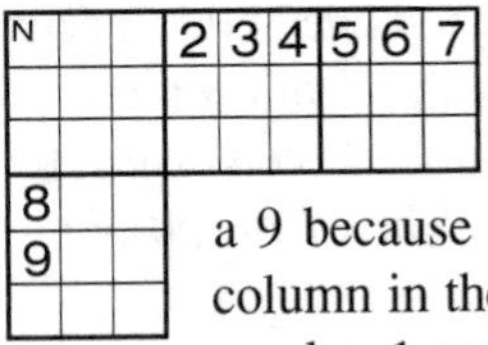

Numbers 1, 8, and 9 are missing from the top row. Cell N cannot contain either an 8 or a 9 because they already appear in the left column in the lower left box. Therefore, the number 1 must be placed in cell N.

Master Pattern 1

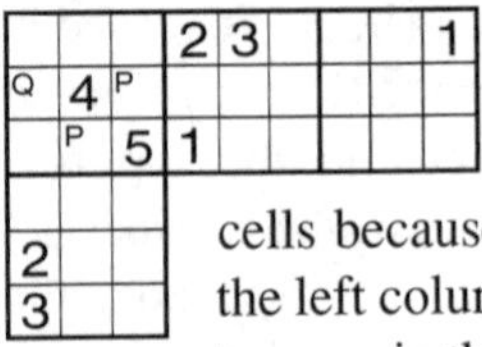

In the upper left box, the numbers 2 and 3 will be placed in each of the two P cells because the appearance of 2 and 3 in the left column in the lower left box and the top row in the middle box negates any other possibility. The number 1 cannot be placed in the top or bottom rows in the upper left box because of the 1s that appear in the top and bottom rows in the middle and far right boxes. Therefore, in the upper left box, the number 1 must be placed in cell Q.

Master Pattern 2

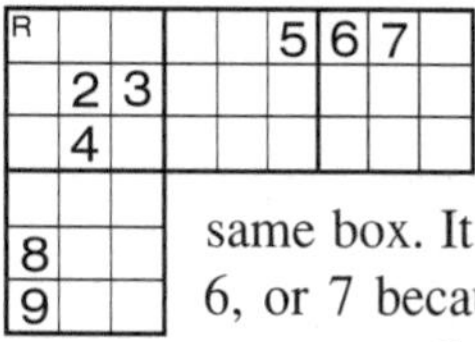

Cell R cannot contain the numbers 2, 3, or 4 because they already appear in the same box. It cannot contain the numbers 5, 6, or 7 because they already appear in the same row. It cannot be the numbers 8 or 9 because they already appear in the same column. Therefore, cell R must contain the number 1. (Note: This deduction may seem simple, but it's easily missed when solving Sudoku!)

Why Handmade?

By Nobuhiko Kanamoto, chief editor, Nikoli

A well-made Sudoku is a pleasure to solve, but there are so many Sudoku puzzles manufactured by computer programs that I would like to explain why we at Nikoli continue to make Sudoku by hand.

Sudoku is a pencil puzzle with simple rules. It's so beautiful, you might fall in love with it. Perhaps you are fascinated already by Sudoku and are yearning for more. If so, do you know how to recognize a truly good Sudoku puzzle?

Let's consider a puzzle that has been made using a computer program. If you are a reasonably experienced solver, you might wish to tackle it. You will soon discover that making a start is difficult. There are no cells in which to place a number using straight-forward techniques.

		4			9			8
	3			5			1	
7			4			2		
3			8			1		
	5						9	
		6			1			2
		8			3			1
	2			4			5	
6			1			7		

2	6	4	3	1	9	5	7	8
8	3	9	2	5	7	4	1	6
7	1	5	4	8	6	2	3	9
3	7	2	8	9	4	1	6	5
4	5	1	6	3	2	8	9	7
9	8	6	5	7	1	3	4	2
5	4	8	7	6	3	9	2	1
1	2	7	9	4	8	6	5	3
6	9	3	1	2	5	7	8	4

I'll show you what to do. Look at box one (we number the boxes from left to right, starting with the top row, so box one is the upper left 3 x 3 square). There is no number 6 in this box, but there are 6s in columns one and three. So, in box one, a 6 can go only in column two, but there are two possible cells. Next, let's look at the number 1. There are no 1s in box four and box seven. But there are 1s in rows four, six, seven, and nine. In box four, a 1 can go only in row five, and in box seven a 1 can go only in row eight. This means that columns one and three cannot be used for a 1 in box one. The two cells of column two in box one will be occupied by a 1 and a 6. Using this information, you can find the cell that contains an 8 in box one. That's right—column one, row two. Now, all of the 8s can be placed easily. Once you have discovered how to solve this problem, the puzzle presents no other difficulties.

Can you really say that you enjoy solving this kind of puzzle? I never can. Computer-generated Sudoku puzzles lack a vital ingredient that makes puzzles enjoyable—the sense of communication between solver and author. The best Sudoku make you concentrate, but aren't stressful. They are absorbing, never boring.

Please don't misunderstand me. I don't mean that a good Sudoku must be easy. A human sensibility is required for fiendish puzzles, too.

Good Sudoku authors are always considering a solver's feelings. Can a computer program do this? Can a computer take into account the way a solver thinks? I am concerned that poor Sudoku, which take no account of solvers, will overwhelm us—and the joy of pure Sudoku will be lost forever.

Why Nikoli?

By Maki Kaji, the "godfather" of Sudoku and the president of Nikoli

We have been supplying handmade Sudoku puzzles for twenty years. We discovered this puzzle twenty-five years ago in one of Dell's puzzle magazines in America. Ever since, we have been absorbed in the never-ending task of creating smart and elegant puzzles.

As you read earlier, we came up with the rule that digits must be arranged in a symmetrical pattern. We think it's a beautiful idea. But during all the time we have been creating the puzzles, we have continued to nurture and develop Sudoku. We continue to think more about the solving process than the end result. This is a question of good taste—an issue that computers will never comprehend.

Nikoli's puzzles are featured in all Japanese newspapers and magazines—100 percent of them! This is because Japanese solvers prefer our Sudoku puzzles. If you stay with Nikoli, you will come to understand the reasons why.

You may invent a program to create Sudoku puzzles, but you will never create Nikoli's Sudoku puzzles. So I will end with one piece of advice: Choose wisely.

PART 1

Easy

Puzzle 1 Easy

1			6			2		
	6		2		4			
		2				8		3
7	5				8		1	
				1				
	4		3				5	6
2		4				1		
			5		3		4	
		3			9			7

Time ________

Puzzle 2 Easy

				7	8			2
		6	3					7
5	3						6	
		1					2	
		5		8		6		
	4					9		
	8						7	4
4					2	3		
1			7	6				

Time __________

Puzzle 3 Easy

				6	9	8		
	4	6	3					
					1		5	
5	1	2						
			4		7			
						6	3	5
	6		1					
					2	9	1	
		4	5	7				

Time __________

Puzzle 4 Easy

	9			2				8
4				7			9	
8			5				2	
			8			1		
		5				6		
		9			2			
	1				4			7
	4			9				6
6				3			1	

Time __________

Puzzle 5 Easy

	5	6			3			
		8	1				7	9
								4
2	8							
	3	9		2		6	8	
							1	7
5								
7	6				8	4		
			2			1	5	

Time __________

Puzzle 6 Easy

	1			7				4
7			8				5	
		8			3	2		
	2			1		8		
8			2		7			3
		5		3			4	
		2	1			7		
	8				9			1
3				4			6	

Time ________

Puzzle 7 Easy

	9	8						4
			9	3				8
					7			
		9	6		4			
7	5						4	1
			5		3	6		
			1					
6				9	5			
3						4	8	

Time ___________

Puzzle 8 Easy

8	5							1
					5	3		6
	4				6	9		
	1	7			9			
			3			8	7	
		8	7				4	
6		2	1					
1							3	5

Time ________

Puzzle 9 Easy

						8	5	
6		1			2			
5			1				3	
	6			1		3		
			5		3			
		5		7			9	
	5				7			6
			2			7		4
	9	2						

Time ________

Puzzle 10 Easy

9	5				4	2		
		2		8				
1		4		2				
	1				2	5		
	7						4	
		8	6				3	
				4		6		9
				7		8		
		9	8				5	7

Time ________

Puzzle 11 Easy

4	5							6
				2				4
		9	8			1	2	
	7				8			
	4						9	
			9				7	
	2	5			4	7		
7				5				
1							6	9

Time ________

Puzzle 12 Easy

2							7	1
			3	1				8
		4	5					
	5	3			8			
	6						1	
			9			3	2	
					9	6		
7				2	5			
6	9							7

Time ________

Puzzle 13 Easy

					2		8	
7		5				4		
	2		6				9	
5				6		2		
			4		8			
		9		3				5
	8				1		3	
		6				7		8
	4		3					

Time ________

Puzzle 14 Easy

	2			4			6	
3			8					4
		5						3
	6				3	1		
	9						8	
		4	6				5	
7						2		
2					9			7
	3			2			4	

Time __________

Puzzle 15 Easy

			2			7	1	
		3			7			8
		1		6				
	3				6	5		
	5						7	
		8	5				9	
				2		4		
1			4			3		
	7	2			8			

Time ________

Puzzle 16 Easy

			4	5				
		4			7	8		
2		6				9		
5			3				9	
	8						6	
	1				4			3
		1				7		5
		3	7			4		
				8	6			

Time ________

Puzzle 17 Easy

							1	5
	4	9						
2			3		1	7		
8			2				9	
	9						7	
	7				6			1
		4	9		5			7
						5	4	
6	1							

Time __________

Puzzle 18 Easy

						6	1	
			4	6				2
4	7				8			9
		1			9			
		2				7		
			5			9		
7			8				3	6
2				9	3			
	5	4						

Time ___________

Puzzle 19 Easy

		1			5			3
6			4			8		
	3			2			7	
1					9			
		3				6		
			8					7
	2			3			1	
		7			8			5
4			5			7		

Time ________

Puzzle 20 Easy

			7				6	
		2		8				4
	4				2		3	
8						5		
	9		6		3		8	
		6						3
	2		5				9	
6				4		2		
	8				1			

Time ________

Puzzle 21 Easy

			4		8			
8		9				1		7
	5			6			8	
		7				5		
			2		1			
		3				8		
	9			3			4	
5		1				6		2
			9		5			

Time ________

Puzzle 22 Easy

		1	2		5	6		
		3	4		7	8		
2	6			8			3	5
1	5			4			7	9
		4	7		1	5		
8	7			9			2	4
3	4			1			6	8
		8	3		4	9		
		9	6		8	2		

Time __________

Puzzle 23 Easy

		8	9			2	6	
	7			8				3
	1			5				
		4			7			
		3				5		
			2			6		
				3			4	
9				6			5	
	5	7			4	9		

Time ________

Puzzle 24 Easy

6	3				5			4
	7			9			2	3
		1	3		2	7		
4		3		1		5		
	9		6		3		4	
		6		7		1		9
		4	8		6	3		
3	2			4			6	
7			9				5	2

Time __________

Puzzle 25 Easy

	3	1			2			
6			5			7		
						1		
	4	6			1			7
7			6		3			8
3			7			4	2	
		5						
		2			6			3
			8			9	5	

Time ________

Puzzle 26 Easy

	1	2	3					
	4	5	6			1	2	3
	7	8	9			4	5	6
						7	8	9
1	2	3						
4	5	6			1	2	3	
7	8	9			4	5	6	
					7	8	9	

Time ___________

Puzzle 27 Easy

	6	2	5				8	1
5	1				4			7
4			8	9				
7				6		8	9	3
		3	1		5	7		
2	8	4		7				6
				1	6			9
3			2				6	4
1	2				9	3	5	

Time __________

Puzzle 28 Easy

1	2						4	5
4			7	6	2			3
		8				9		
	5			8			2	
	1		4		5		7	
	3			7			8	
		7				2		
9			2	3	4			7
2	6						9	1

Time ________

Puzzle 29 Easy

		1	2	3	4	5		
	5						6	
3			6	8	5			7
2		5	8		1	9		4
4		9		5		3		8
1		7	9		3	6		2
7			4	1	6			5
	4						3	
		8	3	9	7	2		

Time ________

Puzzle 30 Easy

5		1				4		9
	3		2		9		8	
2			1		5			3
	1	7	4		8	2	5	
	2	4	3		6	1	9	
9			8		1			5
	4		5		7		6	
7		2				3		8

Time ________

Puzzle 31 Easy

7			5		4			3
	1	3				7	5	
	9		3		7		6	
5		6		2		9		4
			4		6			
1		7		8		6		2
	8		1		9		4	
	5	4				2	1	
3			6		2			5

Time __________

Puzzle 32 Easy

	5						8	
4	1	9				2	7	6
	3			1			9	
			1	2	3			
		3	4		6	8		
			7	8	9			
	8			6			1	
1	2	6				5	4	7
	7						3	

Time __________

Puzzle 33 Easy

7			2		1			9
	4			8			1	
		8		9		6		
3			6		4			1
	8	5		3		7	4	
6			5		8			2
		1		6		2		
	2			4			3	
8			1		5			4

Time ________

Puzzle 34 Easy

5			1		9			6
	8			6			4	
		4				9		
4			8		3			5
	1						9	
6			9		5			1
		7				6		
	3			8			1	
9			2		6			7

Time __________

Puzzle 35 Easy

		4	1		8	5		
		6	9		3	4		
5	8						9	1
2	3						7	5
				1				
7	6						4	8
8	9						6	3
		5	8		2	9		
		2	6		7	8		

Time __________

Puzzle 36 Easy

	7			9			8	
5			4		1			3
		3		2		6		
3	2						5	4
			3		7			
6	5						9	8
		6		8		1		
1			7		5			2
	8			3			7	

Time ________

Puzzle 37 Easy

	7			4			1	
1		2				3		4
	8		5		6		9	
		3		7		1		
6			1		4			7
		9		3		2		
	6		3		7		8	
2		8				5		1
	9			5			2	

Time ________

Puzzle 38 Easy

	7			4	3			
1			9			8		
2		5					4	
3		9			7			5
4		7		1		2		6
5			8			9		7
	6					1		8
		2			5			9
			3	6			2	

Time __________

Puzzle 39 Easy

8				5		7		3
		2		9	1			
5			6				1	
	7		1			3		
9	2			4			7	5
		8			9		2	
	9				2			6
			9	3		1		
4		6		1				8

Time ________

Puzzle 40 Easy

6	9						5	8
7			8					4
		4	7			9		
				1		8	4	
			5	2	8			
	1	7		3				
		1			3	5		
3					6			1
5	2						7	9

Time ________

Puzzle 41 Easy

	9			5		8		
		7			8			4
3			4				1	
	4			6		5		
5			9		1			7
		8		3			9	
	5				2			6
4			8			9		
		3		7			8	

Time ________

Puzzle 42 Easy

		7	3	8	1	9		
			9		6			
6				5				8
5	6		4				1	2
7		4				6		9
1	8				5		7	3
3				6				7
			1		7			
		5	2	4	9	3		

Time __________

Puzzle 43 Easy

	3	5	6		1	9	8	
	4		8		7		2	
	7	4	1	2	3	8	5	
			4		6			
	5	2	7	8	9	6	3	
	8		3		2		6	
	2	1	9		4	5	7	

Time ________

Puzzle 44 Easy

	1						7	
4	7			3			2	9
			1		6			
		8			5	3		
	6			1			8	
		2	7			6		
			3		4			
8	5			9			1	2
	9						5	

Time __________

Puzzle 45 Easy

1			9		3			2
		2		1		4		
	7						9	
6			4		1			8
	2			5			3	
3			6		7			4
	6						1	
		3		9		5		
4			5		2			6

Time ________

Puzzle 46 Easy

	1				2	6		
		2		4				8
		3						2
	4		7		6	8		
1	5			8			7	3
		8	3		4		1	
9						2		
5				3		7		
		4	1				5	

Time __________

Puzzle 47 Easy

6		1		5				
	8		9		6			
9		5		1		2		
	6				7		9	
4		8				1		5
	1		4				2	
		4		2		8		9
			5		9		1	
				6		5		7

Time ________

Puzzle 48 Easy

	5			2			8	9
8	6		9	5				4
					8			
	4				5	1		
1	3						6	8
		7	8				9	
			2					
5				6	1		3	7
3	8			7			2	

Time __________

Puzzle 49 Easy

	1		4		5		6	
3								9
		6		2		3		
7			8		3			2
		8		9		7		
6			7		1			5
		1		8		5		
9								1
	6		9		2		3	

Time ________

Puzzle 50 Easy

		5			2	6		
			4	7			8	
6				3				1
	8				3			4
	6	1				8	5	
2			6				3	
8				4				9
	4			5	9			
		2	3			7		

Time ________

PART 2

Medium

Puzzle 51 Medium

			3	6				7
		1				2		
	9				8		3	
3			1			5		
4								3
		2			9			6
	5		6				1	
		8				6		
2				7	5			

Time ________

Puzzle 52 Medium

		5					9	
					7	6		
		4		1				
	7							1
9			5		8			6
2							4	
				2		7		
		1	9					
	8					3		

Time __________

Puzzle 53 Medium

		2					8	
					6			1
	5			7				
1	8		9					
		4				6		
					3		5	2
				4			9	
2			1					
	3					5		

Time ________

Puzzle 54 Medium

5	1	8						
					6	1	5	
				4				8
			6					2
4			3		7			9
8					1			
9				6				
	2	6	8					
						4	6	3

Time ________

Puzzle 55 Medium

8	3					1	4	
				9	8			
		6	7					
							2	3
		3	2		1	7		
2	6							
					7	2		
			3	4				
	4	5					1	6

Time ________

Puzzle 56 Medium

				6	8	1		
	3	1	7				5	
4								
5					7	6		
	6						2	
		7	5					4
								3
	2				9	7	4	
		8	6	1				

Time __________

Puzzle 57 Medium

	7					6		
		2			3			5
8			7				3	
	1			6		3		
			1		5			
		9		4			5	
	5				4			9
3			9			1		
		7					4	

Time __________

Puzzle 58 Medium

			6					4
		2		7				
	3				1		6	
9				5		8		6
			9		3			
5		1		6				3
	4		5				7	
				8		1		
6					7			

Time ________

Puzzle 59 Medium

5			2			1		
		9			1			
	4			7				8
3			1				8	
		2				4		
	6				9			1
2				3			7	
			4			9		
		8			6			2

Time ________

Puzzle 60 Medium

						6	1	
2	3				7			9
		9		4				
		5		6				
1	9						6	2
				9		5		
				2		8		
3			8				4	5
	6	7						

Time ________

Puzzle 61 Medium

	7				8		5	
1			2			6		
		5		4				8
			9				8	
2								5
	6				2			
4				1		7		
		8			3			9
	3		6				2	

Time ________

Puzzle 62 Medium

	1				4			6
5		6				7		
			1				9	
		2			3			8
	4						3	
9			7			1		
	2				6			
		4				3		5
3			8				4	

Time ________

Puzzle 63 Medium

		3		2				
					6			9
1							4	
	8				5	2		
	9						1	
		7	8				3	
	6							8
5			1					
				3		7		

Time __________

Puzzle 64 Medium

6								9
		2	8					
		3	5			2	6	
				4		8	5	
			6		1			
	1	4		2				
	7	5			8	1		
					3	4		
9								6

Time ________

Puzzle 65 Medium

						7	4	8
	3							
	4		2		5	9	6	
	9		6					
			1		7			
					8		9	
	5	9	3		6		2	
							1	
1	2	6						

Time __________

Puzzle 66 Medium

		1				6		
	2		7			5		
3			5			4		
4				1	6			
	6						8	
			3	8				4
		8			3			1
		2			7		3	
		6				2		

Time ________

Puzzle 67 Medium

		8	5					
	3		7				6	
4			8			7		
6	2	5			1			
			2			5	3	1
		2			3			8
	7				5		1	
					4	6		

Time __________

Puzzle 68 Medium

	4				7			
				8			1	
2						9		
1				4		5		
6								7
		8		3				4
		7						2
	9			1				
			4				6	

Time ________

Puzzle 69 Medium

	3				5	7		
9				7			4	
7			2				1	
			7			2		
		7				1		
		8			2			
	5				9			4
	6			3				8
		2	5				6	

Time __________

Puzzle 70 Medium

6	8					4		
		1					3	9
			7	1				
5					8			
	2	7				5	4	
			4					6
				7	1			
3	4					1		
		8					9	5

Time ________

Puzzle 71 Medium

		4				1		
	5	1			2	7		
			7	3			6	5
			9				3	
	4				3			
4	1			9	5			
		8	2			9	7	
		2				8		

Time ________

Puzzle 72 Medium

				7	1			
9	4			3				5
6							1	2
		3	7					
		8				9		
					6	7		
8	7							1
3				9			4	7
			2	8				

Time ________

Puzzle 73 Medium

7				1		9		2
	8		5					
		4						
	9		8					
1								3
					6		7	
						8		
					4		5	
2		7		3				6

Time __________

Puzzle 74 Medium

			3	7			9	
		3			5			2
	2							4
		9				1	3	
			8		7			
	8	6				5		
5							2	
4			9			6		
	7			1	6			

Time __________

Puzzle 75 Medium

			5					
		8		7		9		
	3				4		8	
		3		2				6
	7		8		9		2	
9				6		1		
	5		4				3	
		7		1		2		
					2			

Time __________

Puzzle 76 Medium

5			6					3
		7			8	5		
	9			2			8	
7					5	2		
		1	2					8
	2			6			7	
		5	7			1		
6					3			9

Time __________

Puzzle 77 Medium

	7			9				
5			7			6		
		8			6			9
	2			5			4	
			2		9			
	3			7			8	
8			1			5		
		2			8			3
				6			9	

Time __________

Puzzle 78 Medium

			2		1			
				5				
	4	1				3	9	
1			7		6			3
9								8
5			9		2			6
	3	6				1	7	
				1				
			6		3			

Time ________

Puzzle 79 Medium

	5			6			8	
7	9						3	5
			5		4			
		1				2		
2								3
		5				4		
			8		7			
1	4						7	2
	6			9			1	

Time ________

Puzzle 80 Medium

2				6				9
	6		1		7		5	
				3				
	9						1	
5		1				8		7
	7						3	
				2				
	1		9		6		7	
8				7				4

Time ________

Puzzle 81 Medium

		3				7		
	4			5			3	
7				1				8
		1				8		
	8		6		5		4	
		2				3		
3				6				9
	2			7			5	
		4				1		

Time ________

Puzzle 82 Medium

	5			2				
		8			3		2	
	1			8				6
4			8				7	
		5				4		
	7				9			3
3				1			9	
	9		5			7		
				4			6	

Time ________

Puzzle 83 Medium

				4				8
		6	7			2	3	
	4				9			
	9				7			
2			1		6			3
			2				6	
			8				2	
	8	9			4	5		
4				6				

Time __________

Puzzle 84 Medium

				3			7	
6	4			8			9	
					9			
		4	5		1			
8	9						2	5
			7		8	3		
			1					
	2			5			8	1
	3			4				

Time ________

Puzzle 85 Medium

		6					4	2
					7		5	
9				8				
		4	2					
	8						1	
					3	9		
				4				5
	5		1					
3	7					6		

Time ________

Puzzle 86 Medium

4						8		
			5		9		2	
		3						4
			7			9		
	5						8	
		6			3			
7						3		
	2		8		4			
		9						6

Time ________

Puzzle 87 Medium

							9	
	9	3	7				5	
	5		6				8	4
	6	1	2					
					4	9	7	
2	3				9		6	
	4				7	3	1	
	7							

Time ________

Puzzle 88 Medium

2	1					5	4	
				1	5			
		9	7					
1	6				3	9		
				9				
		5	1				2	8
					7	6		
			8	2				
	3	7					9	4

Time __________

Puzzle 89 Medium

		4		7		3		
			9		8			
7		5				9		1
	2						9	
4								2
	1						3	
1		2				6		7
			5		9			
		3		1		4		

Time __________

Puzzle 90 Medium

	2	8						9
			3	8			5	
6					1			
3					9	4		
	8						7	
		6	2					1
			8					2
	4			7	5			
1						5	8	

Time ________

Puzzle 91 Medium

		1				3		
6			3		1			7
	2			8			5	
		7				5		
			4		9			
		2				1		
	4			1			6	
3			9		4			5
		9				8		

Time ________

Puzzle 92 Medium

4				9				6
	7		3			9	2	
	1		6					
					2	3		
	4						1	
		7	1					
					1		6	
	5	6			4		9	
9				5				7

Time ________

Puzzle 93 Medium

2			6				4	
	3			7		9		
		6			4			5
			7				5	
		3				6		
	8				5			
6			1			5		
		4		5			2	
	2				3			6

Time __________

Puzzle 94 Medium

	7					4		
			7					8
6		3		8		7		
			1		5		2	
		7				9		
	8		4		7			
		8		6		2		5
2					9			
		4					6	

Time ________

Puzzle 95 Medium

		5		9	1			
		7				4	2	
			8					7
			9					5
	5	2				1	9	
4					6			
1					4			
	6	4				8		
			3	1		9		

Time ________

Puzzle 96 Medium

	5		6		7		3	
		2				9		
7				8				6
	1						9	
		5				2		
	7						4	
3				5				7
		6				1		
	9		4		1		5	

Time ________

Puzzle 97 Medium

4			2		1			8
			4		3			
		7				4		
1	5						3	6
2	3						4	5
		4				9		
			1		5			
3			6		8			7

Time ___________

Puzzle 98 Medium

			6	9	2			
		6				9	2	
		3						8
			8					9
	6	2				5	7	
7					1			
5						1		
	1	8				6		
			1	3	4			

Time ________

Puzzle 99 Medium

	7	5	8	9				
					3			
		4	6			2		
	6			7			2	
1								5
	2			8			3	
		3			4	8		
			9					
				1	6	5	4	

Time ________

Puzzle 100 Medium

	5			6			1	
			5		1			
		7				9		
9			6		2			8
	6						7	
7			4		5			3
		3				6		
			9		8			
	9			2			4	

Time ________

Puzzle 101 Medium

4				3	7	5		
			1					2
		3						9
		1			5		6	
	9						1	
	6		8			7		
9						4		
8					1			
		7	9	4				5

Time ___________

Puzzle 102 Medium

	9		5		3		8	
8								6
			2		4			
7		4				2		1
9		2				3		4
			8		9			
5								7
	7		3		2		6	

Time ________

Puzzle 103 Medium

5			6		3			1
		6				9		
	2			4			6	
		3				5		
			5		1			
		7				6		
	4			7			2	
		5				3		
1			2		4			9

Time ________

Puzzle 104 Medium

		7	5		3	9		
	6						5	
2								4
3				8				6
			4		1			
7				6				8
1								3
	7						4	
		4	3		9	2		

Time ________

Puzzle 105 Medium

		4	8		1	5		
1	3						7	8
		6				4		
	2		4		9		5	
		9				8		
7	6						1	5
		5	6		8	9		

Time ________

Puzzle 106 Medium

			7			3		
		5		3			7	
	1				8			9
5			4			1		
	4			6			5	
		8			9			3
9			2				1	
	7			8		9		
		6			7			

Time ________

Puzzle 107 Medium

6		1		7				
	8		6				9	
		2				7		3
2					1		8	
		6				9		
	1		4					2
3		5				2		
	4				2		5	
				9		6		7

Time ___________

Puzzle 108 Medium

	5	4	3			8		
				7			2	4
				8				
		7	8					
2	6						4	9
					9	1		
				4				
5	3			9				
		2			6	3	5	

Time ________

Puzzle 109 Medium

		9	2			8		
	1			3	4		6	
		3						2
			3				4	
		7				2		
	6				9			
3						6		
	9		5	4			7	
		8			6	4		

Time ________

Puzzle 110 Medium

9	6			8	2			
			3					7
		1					8	
7	8				3	9		
		5	1				4	3
	1					2		
6					7			
			2	3			5	1

Time ________

Puzzle 111 Medium

5					8	2		
4				2			9	
	2			7			1	
		6			5	8		
		4	2			6		
	3			6			7	
	8			5				9
		1	7					3

Time __________

Puzzle 112 Medium

		2				3		
		7				1		
3			8		6			7
4				9				5
	7						3	
9				8				6
8			1		7			4
		3				9		
		5				6		

Time ________

Puzzle 113 Medium

3								5
	7		2	1			8	
		9			4	3		
		7					9	
	4						3	
	1					5		
		5	9			4		
	3			6	8		2	
6								3

Time ________

Puzzle 114 Medium

		5	3				7	
				1	9			
	2	4				1		
3						2		
7			2		6			3
		1						6
		3				6	4	
			8	7				
	1				4	3		

Time __________

Puzzle 115 Medium

			8	3	6			
		8				3		
		5				2		
7	2			6			4	8
4	8			1			3	6
		7				9		
		1				6		
			5	9	7			

Time __________

Puzzle 116 Medium

	1	8					6	5
2			9			8		
				7	5			
	5	6						
			6		7			
						9	4	
			3	1				
		7			2			3
3	2					4	1	

Time __________

Puzzle 117 Medium

		8			3		2	
			7			1		
5				6				
	6							9
	4						3	
1							7	
				8				5
		3			2			
	7		9			6		

Time ________

Puzzle 118 Medium

				4				
		1				2		
	5		6		3		8	
		3	9		4	7		
6								9
		2	3		5	1		
	8		5		7		6	
		9				4		
				1				

Time ________

Puzzle 119 Medium

			8				1	
	5			4			2	
	1			6				9
5					7	2		
	8						5	
		4	5					7
2				7			4	
	4			3			8	
	9				1			

Time ___________

Puzzle 120 Medium

7					6			
	2					7		4
		3		9				
	4		1					
8								5
					3		6	
				2		1		
5		6					3	
			4					9

Time ________

Puzzle 121 Medium

				4				
	4		7		5		6	
		2				8		
	6			5			7	
9			1		3			5
	1			8			4	
		7				2		
	5		4		6		3	
				1				

Time ________

Puzzle 122 Medium

2								6
			3	1				
		4			9	3		
		7	5		2		4	
	6						2	
	3		8		6	5		
		5	1			7		
				4	7			
8								1

Time __________

Puzzle 123 Medium

	4						5	
		3				6		
	1		2		8		3	
6				2				9
	3						2	
1				5				6
	2		3		1		4	
		8				1		
	9						6	

Time ________

Puzzle 124 Medium

		8			4			
2							9	
6			1	3			4	
	3	6			8	7		
		1	2			9	3	
	7			6	5			2
	9							4
			4			8		

Time ________

Puzzle 125 Medium

			9					2
	8	7				5	3	
					7			
4			8	3			9	
3								7
	9			6	2			1
			3					
	5	3				6	7	
9					5			

Time ________

Puzzle 126 Medium

	6	9			2			
7					4		8	
				9				1
		3	5					9
	5						6	
6					1	2		
3				8				
	1		6					2
			9			5	7	

Time ________

Puzzle 127 Medium

	4				6			
5		8		9				4
			3				6	
		5				7		
	9		2		4		3	
		7				8		
	5				8			
3				1		5		6
			9				1	

Time ___________

Puzzle 128 Medium

	2							4
		5	8				6	
		3		2				
			9					1
		7				8		
4					6			
				7		5		
	1				4	3		
6							9	

Time ________

Puzzle 129 Medium

	5						7	
2	7						1	4
			8		9			
		6	1		5	3		
		7	3		8	9		
			5		4			
8	1						6	5
	3						2	

Time ________

Puzzle 130 Medium

	9	5			4	1		
			5				6	
				2				9
					8			3
	2	7				4	9	
4			1					
6				9				
	8				5			
		4	2			3	8	

Time __________

Puzzle 131 Medium

	6	7				2		
3			1	5			9	
							7	
		5	6					3
2								6
1					8	4		
	3							
	4			7	9			2
		9				3	1	

Time ________

Puzzle 132 Medium

8							4	
9			5	2			7	
		1			9	8		
		2					6	
			8		4			
	5					7		
		3	6			9		
	9			7	5			1
	2							7

Time ________

Puzzle 133 Medium

7					3	2	5	
3				8				
		5	9			3		
	6					8		
	4						6	
		8					1	
		4			1	7		
				9				3
	7	1	2					4

Time ________

Puzzle 134 Medium

	1		4	3				
		7			8			3
		4				2	8	
	5							6
6								9
3							1	
	4	6				9		
8			7			6		
				5	9		4	

Time ________

Puzzle 135 Medium

					8	9		
1			7	6			5	
4		5						
	5				2	8		
	2						3	
		9	5				6	
						4		3
	3			7	9			8
		7	2					

Time ________

Puzzle 136 Medium

		2	8					
4	3					6		5
					1			
	5			6				
1								7
				3			2	
			7					
9		3					4	1
					5	8		

Time ___________

Puzzle 137 Medium

	7					8		2
			8				1	
	4			3				
		8	6					
1								9
					2	7		
				4			8	
	2				7			
6		9					5	

Time __________

Puzzle 138 Medium

8	5						7	2
		4				3		
			8		2			
	6			9			5	
		3				7		
	2			4			9	
			4		6			
		2				5		
7	9						8	6

Time ________

Puzzle 139 Medium

4			8		3			
			9			8		
		6					2	
2	9			4				5
			7		9			
1				3			9	7
	2					5		
		8			6			
			4		1			6

Time ________

Puzzle 140 Medium

			4			9		
		6			5		2	
	7			1				8
	3		6					4
		1				2		
4					8		3	
1				3			5	
	4		1			6		
		3			2			

Time ________

Puzzle 141 Medium

			1					
		9	7					
		6	9			5	8	2
		2			4	9	1	
	7	8	2			3		
3	5	7			9	1		
					5	4		
					6			

Time __________

Puzzle 142 Medium

			7	1				
					6	5		
	1	7				8		
	3		8		4			7
8								9
7			5		3		6	
		6				2	4	
		5	1					
				3	8			

Time ________

Puzzle 143 Medium

5					8			2
	6			4		7	3	
	2							
3			4		1			
	1						6	
			6		2			7
							7	
	4	3		8			9	
9			7					5

Time ________

Puzzle 144 Medium

	2	1			7	6		
			9				8	
			3				5	
	6	9			1	2		
		4	2			7	3	
	4				9			
	7				5			
		3	4			9	1	

Time ________

Puzzle 145 Medium

		9			1			
	2			5				6
		4			3		9	
4			9			1		
	7						8	
		3			7			5
	5		7			4		
9				1			3	
			8			2		

Time __________

Puzzle 146 Medium

2					3			1
		5		2				4
	9			4		8		
	8					5		
			2		6			
		3					6	
		6		1			2	
5				7		3		
8			3					7

Time __________

Puzzle 147 Medium

		4		9				6
	9		2				3	
8		6				4		
	4				3			
1								7
			6				5	
		7				3		9
	6				5		1	
3				8		7		

Time ________

Puzzle 148 Medium

	6						3	
	7			9				5
5			8		7			4
			7			5		
		5				2		
		1			3			
2			4		9			6
6				7			1	
	1						2	

Time ________

Puzzle 149 Medium

6	8					1		
				9	2			
		2	3					7
	5							4
		3	9		5	2		
1							8	
8					9	7		
			8	4				
		7					2	6

Time ________

Puzzle 150 Medium

			5	1				
		7			6	9		
		8					1	3
	5				9			8
	3						2	
4			3				6	
9	8					7		
		6	8			5		
				9	1			

Time __________

Puzzle 151 Medium

					5		2	
	7	4				5		
9			8			3		
	4	3			9		8	
	1		6			2	7	
		9			3			2
		6				4	9	
	8		4					

Time __________

Puzzle 152 Medium

9						2		
	2	7			5		9	
				9				6
		9	4					8
	4						5	
1					2	3		
7				2				
	5		3			1	7	
		8						5

Time __________

Puzzle 153 Medium

		3	5					
	4			6				
	8			9		3	2	
					1			9
3			6		8			7
8			2					
	6	1		8			4	
				1			3	
					2	7		

Time __________

Puzzle 154 Medium

2				8			9	
9					6		2	
3					4			1
	7				5			
		4				8		
			3				4	
1			8					2
	6		9					7
	3			1				9

Time __________

Puzzle 155 Medium

	7			5				
					1		8	
	6						7	9
		4						7
			6		3			
9						5		
1	8						3	
	3		7					
				4			2	

Time ________

Puzzle 156 Medium

		8			1	9		
						2		
1	5			2	8			3
7		1						
		6				5		
						4		8
8			4	3			6	7
		7						
		5	9			3		

Time ________

Puzzle 157 Medium

	2			4		1		
		8			1			3
			2				5	
7				6		4		
	3						8	
		1		3				9
	8				9			
3			6			2		
		6		2			7	

Time ________

Puzzle 158 Medium

	4	9						
		2		6	9			
		5			2		4	8
					1			4
2								6
5			3					
7	2		8			3		
			9	1		5		
						4	7	

Time ________

Puzzle 159 Medium

		8	5			6		
	3				4			
					7			4
			2	5				7
	8	7				5	3	
4				1	8			
9			1					
			6				8	
		2			5	9		

Time ________

Puzzle 160 Medium

	4	1	8					
7				3				4
3				6				1
					6	8	5	
	7	2	1					
6				7				3
8				9				7
					4	5	6	

Time ________

Part 3

Hard

Puzzle 161 Hard

		9			4			2
	5			8		4		
8							3	
			2					9
	8			4			6	
7					9			
	9							1
		6		1			2	
3			4			8		

Time __________

Puzzle 162 Hard

				3			8	
	4		7			2		
		5			8		9	
	2			1				
3		4				6		8
				2			5	
	6		9			8		
		9			7		3	
	3			6				

Time __________

Puzzle 163 Hard

						6	2	
3	4				5			9
		5			7			8
		8						
9	7						3	1
						4		
2			1			5		
4			3				7	2
	1	9						

Time ________

Puzzle 164 Hard

			6		1		4	
		5				8		3
	4		5				1	
8		7						9
5						2		1
	2				5		7	
7		6				4		
	5		9		3			

Time ________

Puzzle 165 Hard

				7				9
	6	3	2	1				5
	9							
	3							
	2	1	6		7	3	5	
							4	
							9	
7				3	2	1	6	
1				8				

Time ________

Puzzle 166 Hard

9	6					5		
					5			
		1	9	2			3	
	4				3	1		
8								3
		7	6				8	
	9			4	6	8		
			5					
		2					9	1

Time __________

Puzzle 167 Hard

					4	7		
	5			7			8	
6			2					1
5					3	9		
	9						6	
		4	5					7
8					9			2
	7			8			1	
		3	6					

Time ________

Puzzle 168 Hard

		5			3			
			8	4				6
1							9	
			7				1	
		2				5		
	6				9			
	4							8
7				1	5			
			2			3		

Time ________

Puzzle 169 Hard

		1	4	2				
					9	2		
	3							8
	6		2		8			3
2								9
1			5		6		2	
6							3	
		8	1					
				7	5	9		

Time __________

Puzzle 170 Hard

			1					
		2	5				7	
	8	5				9	4	
	1				3	5		
			8		4			
		9	2				3	
	3	8				6	5	
	4				1	8		
					9			

Time ________

Puzzle 171 Hard

6			2				9	
	5		3				4	
	9			5				1
		7			9			
		8				9		
			8			5		
4				6			7	
	1				4		3	
	7				8			6

Time ________

Puzzle 172 Hard

			9		3			
	2	1				3	7	
				1				
5			2		7			9
		8				4		
2			5		9			6
				6				
	4	6				5	8	
			8		1			

Time ________

Puzzle 173 Hard

		9			3			
	7			1			8	
5			2			6		
		3			8			5
	4						1	
9			6			2		
		2			1			8
	3			2			5	
			5			1		

Time ________

Puzzle 174 Hard

5			6			7		
		8		5	7		9	
		2					3	
	8							2
2								7
3							5	
	9					6		
	5		9	1		4		
		7			4			9

Time ________

Puzzle 175 Hard

					7			9
		4		1				
8							5	
4					3	8		
	1						7	
		9	5					4
	7							3
				6		2		
3			8					

Time ________

Puzzle 176 Hard

				7	4			
						4	9	
		3	2					6
	5			8	7			1
	2						6	
6			1	4			7	
3					8	7		
	8	9						
			5	6				

Time ________

Puzzle 177 Hard

		8			5	4		
			8					9
9				2			1	
	6				7	5		
4								7
		5	6				3	
	5			3				4
8					9			
		9	2			6		

Time ________

Puzzle 178 Hard

				9	5			
						7	2	
		9	4					5
	2			1	9			6
	3						7	
1			5	7			8	
5					6	3		
	1	8						
			3	2				

Time ________

Puzzle 179 Hard

			2	8				7
		7						9
		4				1	6	
9	5				3			
			9		1			
			6				4	2
	1	3				6		
4						2		
5				3	4			

Time __________

Puzzle 180 Hard

8	9	4						7
			3	9				6
				2				8
					5	1	7	
	5	3	4					
3				5				
1				8	2			
7						2	6	1

Time ________

Puzzle 181 Hard

8					3	7	2	
			5	2				4
		3						
	8				4		9	
	6						8	
	3		1				5	
						2		
9				5	6			
	4	2	7					6

Time __________

Puzzle 182 Hard

	6			1				
	7						2	3
		3			4	5		
		1		6				
4			8		9			5
				2		4		
		6	7			2		
2	9						6	
				5			9	

Time ________

Puzzle 183 Hard

			1					7
5		6					2	
					8			
				5			4	
		3	6		2	8		
	1			9				
			3					
	2					1		9
4					7			

Time ________

Puzzle 184 Hard

						8		
				6			9	1
		7			3	4		
9			7	4				
	4	5				6	2	
				2	9			8
		1	2			5		
6	3			8				
		2						

Time ___________

Puzzle 185 Hard

8								
	6					4		
			7	2			5	
		5	8				2	
		4				1		
	9				1	3		
	3			4	6			
		2					7	
								8

Time __________

Puzzle 186 Hard

4			5					7
	8			7			5	
		7			9	2		
			9				2	
8		2				6		4
	3				7			
		8	7			1		
	2			6			4	
7					2			3

Time _________

Puzzle 187 Hard

					5	6		
						9	2	
2	4			9	8			
	2	6			4	8		
		8	3			5	1	
			1	5			7	3
	9	4						
		3	2					

Time ________

Puzzle 188 Hard

				4	2			
		8	3			9		
	5						4	
3			9	2			6	
		7				5		
	2			1	5			9
	1						7	
		4			6	1		
			2	9				

Time ________

Puzzle 189 Hard

	4						9	
1								7
			8	4	3			
		5		7		6		
		9	4		2	5		
		8		9		3		
			6	1	5			
7								1
	3						2	

Time ________

Puzzle 190 Hard

4			1	5				
	5				4	2		
	3						1	
6							4	
		5	7		1	9		
	2							8
	6						3	
		9	8				6	
				1	9			5

Time __________

Puzzle 191 Hard

	1			7			9	
6		9			2	8		
			6					
	8			3				
1		3				2		6
				2			1	
					9			
		5	2			7		9
	3			5			4	

Time ________

Puzzle 192 Hard

4					8		2	
6			9					1
		8	3			5		
					9	3		
8								9
		6	1					
		7			4	1		
9					2			7
	5		7					4

Time __________

Puzzle 193 Hard

	5					7		
2				8				
		4	1					3
	9					2		
			4		5			
		1					7	
7					2	5		
				9				6
		3					8	

Time ________

Puzzle 194 Hard

	4					8	5	
		3	6					1
2				4				
					3			9
	5	6				1	3	
7			5					
				3				4
8					2	6		
	9	1					8	

Time ___________

Puzzle 195 Hard

								9
		3	6			4		
	7	8			4	2		
	8			9	7			6
9			3	8			5	
		6	2			3	7	
		1			5	6		
3								

Time ________

Puzzle 196 Hard

5				4	2			
		3	9			8		
	9						3	
	7				3			9
2								6
8			1				7	
	2						9	
		5			9	4		
			6	2				5

Time __________

Puzzle 197 Hard

		2	4					
	3						9	
4			9	7				6
		3			8			5
	4						7	
6			5			2		
9				4	3			7
	1						2	
					7	8		

Time ________

Puzzle 198 Hard

		7	1	3				
5					9	4	1	
2								
9				5	6	2		
		8	9	1				5
								9
	1	3	6					7
				8	1	5		

Time ________

Puzzle 199 Hard

						3		
	4		6			1		
	9		1		5			7
		3			4			8
		5				7		
1			2			6		
6			3		7		4	
		7			2		9	
		2						

Time ________

Puzzle 200 Hard

2	3						5	1
		7						
			5	4				
			1	2			3	9
		9				8		
6	4			9	7			
				8	2			
						4		
9	5						1	3

Time ___________

Puzzle 201 Hard

4					2			
	8			9				3
		2	6				9	
						4		8
	7		1		9		6	
1		6						
	9				5	8		
7				2			4	
			8					5

Time ________

Puzzle 202 Hard

		7	9					6
8						3		
	2							
		4	6		7			
	5						2	
			8		3	1		
							8	
		9						4
1					2	9		

Time ________

Puzzle 203 Hard

					8	9		
8				5			6	
3			1				8	
	7	5			3	2		
		9	8			6	3	
	8				5			7
	6			2				1
		7	4					

Time __________

Puzzle 204 Hard

		2	9				6	
	9			7				2
		7						4
			8			6	9	
			5		2			
	3	5			1			
1						5		
2				3			7	
	8				7	1		

Time __________

Puzzle 205 Hard

		2			5			3
		6				1		
4			6			2		
	6		5				1	
3								8
	9				7		3	
		5			1			6
		3				7		
6			4			9		

Time __________

Puzzle 206 Hard

		6	4	7				5
1	2							
					8	3		
		7	5				8	
	4						7	
	1				4	6		
		9	1					
							6	7
6				5	2	1		

Time __________

Puzzle 207 Hard

			4	2	5			
		1				4		
	5						6	
5				7				2
	7		1		6		5	
6				3				9
	6						2	
		5				3		
			9	8	3			

Time ________

Puzzle 208 Hard

		8	5				9	2
				1	4			
3	1					6		
		6			9			
	9						7	
			3			9		
		2					4	5
			7	2				
6	7				8	3		

Time ________

Puzzle 209 Hard

		3						6
			8		2		7	
5								
6					3	5		
	2						9	
		1	6					4
								8
	7		9		1			
8						3		

Time __________

Puzzle 210 Hard

	3							5
8					3		7	
		2		6		1		
	9		1					
7				8				6
					7		2	
		1		9		4		
	7		5					9
9							8	

Time ________

Puzzle 211 Hard

5				1				
	6				4			
		7		6		5	2	
	1		9					8
2								7
4					5		3	
	2	4		7		6		
			3				9	
				9				1

Time ________

Puzzle 212 Hard

				9				
3	7				5		4	
		1			8			7
		5			6			4
		2				9		
7			9			2		
8			5			1		
	6		2				5	8
				3				

Time __________

Puzzle 213 Hard

	6						5	
1				4				9
			3		8			
		3	5		9	4		
	8						1	
		7	8		3	2		
			6		2			
4				9				7
	5						8	

Time ________

Puzzle 214 Hard

		6	8				2	4
9				4				
8				3				
	8				6	9		
	2						8	
		1	4				7	
				7				3
				6				1
5	7				9	4		

Time __________

Puzzle 215 Hard

		3	6				7	
	5			7				9
						8		
8			2		6		5	
7								2
	9		3		7			4
		4						
5				1			6	
	8				2	1		

Time ________

Puzzle 216 Hard

	8						3	
1				9		2		4
	4		5		1			
		1				9		
	7						4	
		2				7		
			8		9		2	
7		6		3				1
	3						7	

Time __________

Puzzle 217 Hard

	6							8
		3		1				
			4			2		
	2			9				7
			5		3			
4				8			1	
		8			7			
				6		4		
2							5	

Time ________

Puzzle 218 Hard

8	4						6	
			6					8
		7			5			9
		3			2			5
	8						9	
9			1			4		
7			9			2		
4					8			
	2						7	3

Time ________

Puzzle 219 Hard

					5			8
	3						2	
		7		1				
3	4				8			
		9				6		
			2				7	5
				7		3		
	6						1	
2			9					

Time ________

Puzzle 220 Hard

	4				9			
5			6		1			
2			3			8		
	6					5		
	2		4		7		9	
		7					1	
		8			3			2
			7		8			3
			1				4	

Time __________

Puzzle 221 Hard

					4	7		
1				6			5	
9			5				1	
	6	8			3			9
7			9			4	3	
	2				5			6
	4			2				1
		3	4					

Time ________

Puzzle 222 Hard

	3				4		9	
6			9					8
		4		8				
	9				3			4
		2				5		
7			4				8	
				5		4		
8					9			3
	7		6				1	

Time __________

Puzzle 223 Hard

		5		1				
	2		9		3		7	
								4
	6			7			2	
7			1		5			8
	9			2			1	
9								
	3		8		4		5	
				6		3		

Time __________

Puzzle 224 Hard

			6	9				
					1	4		
	8	6					5	3
6			1			2		
		9				1		
		5			4			8
8	5					7	6	
		4	7					
				4	3			

Time ________

Puzzle 225 Hard

		7	4				2	
	3			9				7
				8			4	
		6	1					
7	9						3	4
					2	8		
	8			6				
2				1			9	
	4				5	3		

Time ________

Puzzle 226 Hard

	4				2			8
	6				9			3
8				6			7	
			4			9		
		3				4		
		9			8			
	7			3				4
3			9				1	
5			2				6	

Time ___________

Puzzle 227 Hard

	5			3			4	
4								8
		7	1		2	9		
	3						8	
6								1
	9						7	
		6	9		5	2		
1								7
	2			7			3	

Time ________

Puzzle 228 Hard

			7		8			
		2				3		
	5			1			4	
9				5				6
		8	3		9	5		
5				2				1
	1			6			9	
		3				1		
			4		1			

Time ___________

Puzzle 229 Hard

9	5						6	3
		6	1		9	5		
4				1				8
		7				9		
5				6				1
		4	8		7	1		
6	9						2	5

Time ________

Puzzle 230 Hard

			5		1			
		3				7		
	8			9			4	
6			7		8			5
		1				2		
9			2		4			1
	5			3			8	
		2				3		
			6		9			

Time ____________

Puzzle 231 Hard

			2			7	3	
	7	1			3			
4					7			
1				6			9	
	8						5	
	3			1				4
			9					1
			8			9	7	
	4	5			2			

Time ________

Puzzle 232 Hard

		4				1		
			8		6			
2				1		4		7
	8		9				1	
		7				2		
	3				5		4	
9		6		2				8
			5		3			
		3				5		

Time ________

Puzzle 233 Hard

		2	1					
					3	4		
6		8	9				3	
7		3			9		4	
	4		7			8		2
	6				5	3		8
		9	4					
					6	5		

Time ________

Puzzle 234 Hard

	9				4			5
				1	6	7		
		1			8			
	6	3	9					
		9				2		
					2	3	8	
			8			9		
		2	1	5				
7			2				4	

Time ________

Puzzle 235 Hard

	8			3				4
2					5			
	9							1
	4					7		
			1		6			
		8					5	
3							6	
			9					2
5				7			3	

Time ________

Puzzle 236 Hard

1				2				
	9					6		4
					3	7		
			5			3		
	4						1	
		2			7			
		3	7					
6		5					8	
				9				2

Time ________

Puzzle 237 Hard

			2	1				
		2	4					
	3	1					8	2
						3	5	
		3	6		2	1		
	9	8						
7	6					5	3	
					5	7		
				4	1			

Time ________

Puzzle 238 Hard

		8			9		1	
	3				5			6
2				3				
			3				7	4
		2				5		
7	8				1			
				4				3
3			7				9	
	7		1			8		

Time ________

Puzzle 239 Hard

				4	5			
		3					8	9
		2				7		
	9			7	3			1
5								3
1			2	5			9	
		9				6		
7	4					9		
			6	1				

Time ________

Puzzle 240 Hard

			1					7
		4		6			2	
	1			5			4	
	4		9			7		
		6				5		
		2			3		8	
	7			3			5	
	3			8		4		
1					4			

Time ________

Puzzle 241 Hard

					8	5		
			3	1				
7						4	1	
		6		7	9			
2	4						7	5
			2	3		1		
	6	8						2
				9	5			
		9	8					

Time ________

Puzzle 242 Hard

7								8
					2	6	1	
		5	7	6				
2	3				6	1		
		8	1				9	5
				1	7	3		
	4	7	2					
6								1

Time ________

Puzzle 243 Hard

	5						9	
9				1				2
8			7		6			1
			9		2			
		3				8		
			4		8			
1			3		5			6
5				6				4
	9						2	

Time ________

Puzzle 244 Hard

							1	3
				3	5	2		
	4	5	1					
					2	6	7	
9								8
	8	7	5					
					3	1	4	
		9	8	4				
6	7							

Time __________

Puzzle 245 Hard

5					7			4
9						1	2	
		6	3					
	6				1	4		
	8						5	
		1	9				3	
					3	6		
	3	4						8
7			2					3

Time __________

Puzzle 246 Hard

			2			3	1	
		7	1		6	2		
	3	1		6	7			
	9						3	
			3	1		6	5	
		2	7		4	9		
	8	4			9			

Time ___________

Puzzle 247 Hard

	9	5						
			2			4	1	
			7		6			9
	6	7			3			1
2			4			3	9	
3			5		8			
	4	8			9			
						6	2	

Time ________

Puzzle 248 Hard

	2				5			
	4			7				8
1			4				3	
8			5				7	
		5				4		
	6				1			2
	9				6			5
3				9			8	
			8				1	

Time __________

Puzzle 249 Hard

	5			6			2	
4		9				7		3
				1				
		8				3		
9			2		8			6
		4				1		
				8				
2		3				5		8
	4			5			1	

Time ________

Puzzle 250 Hard

			5		7			
	8			1			3	
1								5
		1				8		
9	2		4		1		5	6
		5				3		
7								1
	6			5			9	
			2		8			

Time ________

Puzzle 251 Hard

	3	6						
			8			3	6	
4			5		6			
1					3			
	8	2				7	5	
			1					9
			3		8			7
	2	1			4			
						5	9	

Time ________

Puzzle 252 Hard

			6					8
	4					1		
		3		2	5			
1						9		
	7						3	
		9						5
			9	4		7		
		5					6	
8					2			

Time ________

Puzzle 253 Hard

		8			2	3		
		2					7	9
	3		6					
	2		5					
5		9				4		8
					3		1	
					5		9	
4	8					1		
		1	4			5		

Time ________

Puzzle 254 Hard

			8	9				
	9	2			7	8		
6							1	
		8				1		6
			2		4			
3		6				5		
	7							1
		5	7			3	2	
				4	8			

Time ___________

Puzzle 255 Hard

		4	7					
					5	4		
	2	9			8	3		6
	3	1						9
9						6	8	
5		8	4			1	9	
		2	5					
					3	7		

Time ________

Puzzle 256 Hard

	2			1			4	
8				7				6
					3	1		
			7			4		
5	9						1	3
		8			5			
		2	3					
7				4				8
	8			9			7	

Time __________

Puzzle 257 Hard

					2	7		
		1		3			2	
	9				5			6
			5			2		7
	1						8	
9		8			6			
4			7				3	
	7			9		8		
		6	3					

Time ________

Puzzle 258 Hard

	7			1	2			3
1			9				5	
						6		
	1		4					9
9								7
8					5		1	
		3						
	9				3			8
6			5	7			4	

Time ________

Puzzle 259 Hard

			6		7			
		5		8		1		
	4						9	
8			1		2			5
	3						2	
6			3		9			7
	9						4	
		3		4		2		
			5		8			

Time ________

Puzzle 260 Hard

		3						4
				1			2	
5			9			8		
	1		7				6	
	4				5		8	
		8			3			5
	2			6				
7						4		

Time ________

Puzzle 261 Hard

		9			5			
	6			4		7		
2			7				1	
	2				3			8
		6				5		
4			5				9	
	9				4			3
		3		9			7	
			8			6		

Time ________

Puzzle 262 Hard

		6						
		3			6	8		
	9			4			5	1
	4			6				
		8	4		2	5		
				8			2	
2	6			5			4	
		5	7			1		
						3		

Time ________

Puzzle 263 Hard

			1	8				6
		3						1
		7			5	9		
	7				4	8		
	3						2	
		6	2				7	
		8	7			5		
7						2		
5				6	1			

Time ________

Puzzle 264 Hard

	5					9		
	9		2	1		7		
		8			7			
		7			9			
9	3						8	2
			8			1		
			5			4		
		5		4	8		6	
		2					3	

Time ___________

Puzzle 265 Hard

4				9			2	
	6				4			1
		9			6			
			9			6	1	
5								8
	3	1			2			
			5			7		
6			7				5	
	4			8				2

Time ________

Puzzle 266 Hard

					9		7	
9	1				5		6	
		7				2		
7	8		1				2	
	5				6		8	3
		4				3		
	6		8				9	4
	9		3					

Time __________

Puzzle 267 Hard

				5				
	6	9				1	4	
	2	1				8	3	
			1		2			
3								9
			8		7			
	4	8				3	5	
	5	2				6	7	
				4				

Time ________

Puzzle 268 Hard

	5		6		3			
		7				2		3
	3			4			1	
	6							7
		4		1		9		
1							2	
	7			6			8	
2		5				4		
			7		4		9	

Time __________

Puzzle 269 Hard

		3	9					7
7	4							5
					2		8	
		2			3		9	
		6				2		
	1		4			7		
	8		5					
6							4	9
9					8	6		

Time ________

Puzzle 270 Hard

		4	3					
	7			8		9	5	
				1				2
			9					1
	2	9				6	4	
3					5			
5				4				
	8	1		7			3	
					6	8		

Time __________

PART 4

Very Hard

Puzzle 271 Very Hard

		3	8		9	4		
	4			1			7	
7			1		2			4
		9				1		
8			3		6			2
	2			6			9	
		5	7		3	6		

Time ________

Puzzle 272 Very Hard

		6	1					
1	4							8
				4	8			2
		9	3				5	
	6						4	
	8				5	2		
2			6	7				
6							8	1
					9	5		

Time ________

Puzzle 273 Very Hard

		1	7				3	
	8			9				5
	7				1			9
		6	2		5			
			9		4	7		
1			4				5	
7				8			6	
	3				2	8		

Time ________

Puzzle 274 Very Hard

		7	3				4	
								6
9		6			5	1		
4			8		9	5		
		5	2		3			7
		2	1			7		3
8								
	9				7	4		

Time __________

Puzzle 275 Very Hard

8						5		
	1				6		4	
		5		3				9
2						8		
	9		2		4		3	
		1						5
7				8		4		
	6		5				1	
		4						2

Time ________

Puzzle 276 Very Hard

4					8	3		
		1		9				
	3		4					1
		8	6					3
	6						5	
7					3	1		
6					9		7	
				7		8		
		9	5					4

Time ________

Puzzle 277 Very Hard

9	2			8	5			
			1				5	
			3				2	
	9	7						3
8								4
5						6	9	
	6				7			
	3				8			
			9	4			8	2

Time __________

Puzzle 278 Very Hard

			7					
3						2	4	
8	2				3	5		
	6	1			7			3
9			5			4	7	
		8	3				1	9
	3	7						6
					8			

Time ________

Puzzle 279 Very Hard

	2	6						
7			4	9				
		5			8	7		
				8			4	2
		3				6		
5	1			6				
		1	3			8		
				2	5			3
						4	6	

Time ________

Puzzle 280 Very Hard

	3		1		8			
1			5			3		
		4					5	
8	1				6			7
7			9				4	2
	2					8		
		6			3			5
			4		5		7	

Time __________

Puzzle 281 Very Hard

	9							
3					7	2	4	
5				4				9
	1							7
		5	2		4	6		
9							8	
2				7				3
	7	8	6					5
							6	

Time ________

Puzzle 282 Very Hard

	5			1			2	
		3			4		7	
		8			9			1
			5				9	
		5				7		
	3				6			
1			4			9		
	6		8			3		
	8			2			1	

Time ________

Puzzle 283 Very Hard

				2	6	4	7	
4	7				1		9	
1								
7	8							
2								6
							1	3
								7
	5		8				2	9
	4	3	2	7				

Time ________

Puzzle 284 Very Hard

		7	8		2	1		
	8			1			6	5
					4	8		
1	6						2	9
		3	5					
5	3			9			8	
		9	4		7	3		

Time ________

Puzzle 285 Very Hard

		9	6					
					5	7		
	4	5					8	3
							1	4
		4	9		1	3		
7	3							
6	5					8	3	
		7	1					
					8	5		

Time __________

Puzzle 286 Very Hard

9	4							7
								8
		5	7	9				2
	9				8		1	
	7						6	
	1		2				5	
7				3	1	9		
6								
4							7	5

Time ________

Puzzle 287 Very Hard

	4	9						
			6			4	7	
			4		8			3
		8			5			7
		1				9		
6			3			5		
9			5		2			
	6	7			1			
						1	9	

Time ___________

Puzzle 288 Very Hard

5	3							2
				5	4			7
		8	9					
	5				8	1		
	8						3	
		2	6				4	
					2	5		
6			7	3				
1							2	9

Time ________

Puzzle 289 Very Hard

			5		8			
	6	4				8	7	
8								9
4				1				3
		8				2		
3				7				6
9								2
	3	5				6	9	
			6		1			

Time __________

Puzzle 290 Very Hard

				1	9			
			6			4	9	
2			5					3
	7			6				5
	2						7	
6				9			8	
5					7			2
	4	9			8			
			3	5				

Time ________

Puzzle 291 Very Hard

		7	3					
	4			6				5
		8			4		9	
			6	2			4	
4								8
	3			4	7			
	5		7			2		
6				1			7	
					9	3		

Time ________

Puzzle 292 Very Hard

				3	6	7		
	2							
		9	5			4		8
		3	8					5
4								7
9					7	2		
1		4			3	6		
							1	
		2	9	5				

Time ________

Puzzle 293 Very Hard

1	9				2			
		5	8	6				
						7	3	
	5	1			3			
3			5		4			1
			9			5	2	
	8	7						
				9	7	8		
			2				7	5

Time __________

Puzzle 294 Very Hard

		3	2					
		5	1			4		
	8						3	2
			7		8		5	4
2	1		9		5			
9	4						6	
		8			7	3		
					9	8		

Time ________

Puzzle 295 Very Hard

		7						
	8	3		4				
			9	5		2		
					7	5		6
5	1						7	9
6		8	5					
		5		6	4			
				2		9	6	
						3		

Time __________

Puzzle 296 Very Hard

3		8				1		9
			8		9			
4								6
	6			2			7	
			1		3			
	5			8			9	
1								3
			6		5			
5		9				2		4

Time ___________

Puzzle 297 Very Hard

	6	1	9					
				2	5	3		
7								5
6			4				7	
		2				8		
	9				6			1
9								6
		5	3	6				
					8	1	2	

Time ________

Puzzle 298 Very Hard

				8				
5			3		1			8
		8				7		
	9			7			3	
		6	2		5	9		
	4			1			5	
		3				1		
1			9		4			3
				2				

Time ________

Puzzle 299 Very Hard

		4	6		9	8		
				5				
7		3				6		1
8								2
	2						3	
1								7
6		8				7		4
				6				
		1	8		4	9		

Time ________

Puzzle 300 Very Hard

				8	6			
	9					4		
4		8	1			7		
5				2			7	
	1						8	
	2			3				9
		2			5	9		3
		9					1	
			8	7				

Time __________

Puzzle 301 Very Hard

			5					
		5		3			6	
	3			2		7		8
4					3			7
	6						8	
5			1					4
6		2		8			3	
	4			5		9		
					7			

Time __________

Puzzle 302 Very Hard

			1					5
4			6					2
	6			5			1	
	7				3	4		
5								1
		3	5				2	
	2			7			9	
8					9			4
9					2			

Time ________

Puzzle 303 Very Hard

		3						1
		2		6				8
	9			1		4		
	7		4			9		
			6		2			
		6			1		7	
		9		5			8	
2				4		1		
6						3		

Time __________

Puzzle 304 Very Hard

	9		6					
7				9				8
1					4		5	
		1			5		8	
		2				3		
	4		7			1		
	3		8					7
9				2				4
					7		6	

Time ________

Puzzle 305 Very Hard

		8		7				
	2			3			1	
	6		4				8	
2			3			5		
		9				8		
		3			6			9
	7				9		5	
	3			1			7	
				5		6		

Time __________

Puzzle 306 Very Hard

	6	4					2	1
5			9					
				7	4			
			8			4		
1	4						5	6
		7			2			
			7	5				
					8			9
8	2					1	4	

Time ________

Puzzle 307 Very Hard

			2				7	6
		1	7					
8		9			4	3		
7						8	4	
	2	3						5
		2	4			9		3
					6	5		
6	8				3			

Time ________

Puzzle 308 Very Hard

8			2			6		
6			5			9		
		7			6			8
	5			1			9	
	3			4			1	
2			4			7		
		3			2			5
		8			1			2

Time ________

Puzzle 309 Very Hard

		2	3					
6	9				1	2		
				7			1	
			1					7
5			7		8			4
3					9			
	6			8				
		8	5				7	9
					2	1		

Time ___________

Puzzle 310 Very Hard

		2	4					3
	9			8			4	
		4	1				6	
							5	
		3	2		6	1		
	4							
	5				9	8		
	3			5			1	
7					4	3		

Time ________

Puzzle 311 Very Hard

		5	3				8	
		4		5			9	
	2				6	7		
7					8			
5								3
			9					4
		2	8				6	
	3			4		2		
	1				7	9		

Time ________

Puzzle 312 Very Hard

		9	8				6	
				1			5	4
3				6				
7					8			
	1	8				6	2	
			3					9
				8				2
4	5			3				
	7				2	1		

Time ________

Puzzle 313 Very Hard

		7				3		
	8						5	
2			9		3			4
	4			5			9	
		8				1		
	3			6			7	
3			6		7			9
	2						4	
		6				8		

Time __________

Puzzle 314 Very Hard

				4		8		
	4		1				5	
		5			7			6
5			2			3		
	8						9	
		6			1			2
4			8			5		
	7				2		6	
		3		1				

Time ________

Puzzle 315 Very Hard

					7	3		
			5	1			8	
	7	6						5
					1			3
	5	2				4	9	
3			8					
8						9	4	
	3			2	9			
		1	6					

Time __________

Puzzle 316 Very Hard

		1			9			
				4			2	
3			5			6		
	4		6				8	
	7				1		3	
		3			6			9
	2			8				
			7			1		

Time ________

Puzzle 317 Very Hard

		5			4			
		9			8		3	
			6			8		1
			2			6		9
	2						8	
1		7			9			
5		1			7			
	4		8			5		
			5			4		

Time ________

Puzzle 318 Very Hard

			2		5			
		1				9		
	4			7			6	
9			6		7			5
		4				7		
8			3		1			2
	7			5			4	
		3				1		
			8		9			

Time ________

Puzzle 319 Very Hard

8			2	5				7
		1			7			
	6					9		
4			1				5	
1								2
	5				3			8
		9					4	
			9			7		
2				6	8			9

Time __________

Puzzle 320 Very Hard

	3	9						
4				1	9	7		
			4				5	
			1					2
7		5				8		3
1					6			
	8				3			
		1	9	7				4
						9	8	

Time ________

Solutions

1

1	3	5	6	8	7	2	9	4
9	6	8	2	3	4	5	7	1
4	7	2	9	5	1	8	6	3
7	5	9	4	6	8	3	1	2
3	2	6	7	1	5	4	8	9
8	4	1	3	9	2	7	5	6
2	9	4	8	7	6	1	3	5
6	1	7	5	2	3	9	4	8
5	8	3	1	4	9	6	2	7

2

9	1	4	6	7	8	5	3	2
8	2	6	3	5	1	4	9	7
5	3	7	4	2	9	8	6	1
3	6	1	9	4	5	7	2	8
2	9	5	1	8	7	6	4	3
7	4	8	2	3	6	9	1	5
6	8	2	5	9	3	1	7	4
4	7	9	8	1	2	3	5	6
1	5	3	7	6	4	2	8	9

3

3	5	1	7	6	9	8	4	2
8	4	6	3	2	5	7	9	1
9	2	7	8	4	1	3	5	6
5	1	2	9	3	6	4	8	7
6	8	3	4	5	7	1	2	9
4	7	9	2	1	8	6	3	5
2	6	8	1	9	4	5	7	3
7	3	5	6	8	2	9	1	4
1	9	4	5	7	3	2	6	8

4

5	9	3	4	2	1	7	6	8
4	2	6	3	7	8	5	9	1
8	7	1	5	6	9	4	2	3
2	3	4	8	5	6	1	7	9
7	8	5	9	1	3	6	4	2
1	6	9	7	4	2	8	3	5
9	1	2	6	8	4	3	5	7
3	4	7	1	9	5	2	8	6
6	5	8	2	3	7	9	1	4

5

9	5	6	4	7	3	8	2	1
4	2	8	1	6	5	3	7	9
3	7	1	8	9	2	5	6	4
2	8	7	6	5	1	9	4	3
1	3	9	7	2	4	6	8	5
6	4	5	3	8	9	2	1	7
5	1	2	9	4	6	7	3	8
7	6	3	5	1	8	4	9	2
8	9	4	2	3	7	1	5	6

6

2	1	9	5	7	6	3	8	4
7	3	4	8	2	1	9	5	6
6	5	8	4	9	3	2	1	7
9	2	3	6	1	4	8	7	5
8	4	6	2	5	7	1	9	3
1	7	5	9	3	8	6	4	2
4	6	2	1	8	5	7	3	9
5	8	7	3	6	9	4	2	1
3	9	1	7	4	2	5	6	8

7

1	9	8	2	5	6	7	3	4
4	6	7	9	3	1	2	5	8
5	2	3	4	8	7	9	1	6
2	3	9	6	1	4	8	7	5
7	5	6	8	2	9	3	4	1
8	4	1	5	7	3	6	9	2
9	7	2	1	4	8	5	6	3
6	8	4	3	9	5	1	2	7
3	1	5	7	6	2	4	8	9

8

8	5	6	9	3	7	4	2	1
7	2	9	4	1	5	3	8	6
3	4	1	8	2	6	9	5	7
4	1	7	5	8	9	2	6	3
9	8	3	6	7	2	5	1	4
2	6	5	3	4	1	8	7	9
5	9	8	7	6	3	1	4	2
6	3	2	1	5	4	7	9	8
1	7	4	2	9	8	6	3	5

9

4	2	3	7	6	9	8	5	1
6	8	1	3	5	2	4	7	9
5	7	9	1	8	4	6	3	2
2	6	7	9	1	8	3	4	5
9	4	8	5	2	3	1	6	7
3	1	5	4	7	6	2	9	8
1	5	4	8	3	7	9	2	6
8	3	6	2	9	5	7	1	4
7	9	2	6	4	1	5	8	3

10

9	5	3	7	6	4	2	8	1
7	6	2	5	8	1	3	9	4
1	8	4	3	2	9	7	6	5
3	1	6	4	9	2	5	7	8
2	7	5	1	3	8	9	4	6
4	9	8	6	5	7	1	3	2
8	3	7	2	4	5	6	1	9
5	4	1	9	7	6	8	2	3
6	2	9	8	1	3	4	5	7

11

4	5	2	7	1	9	8	3	6
8	1	7	6	2	3	9	5	4
3	6	9	8	4	5	1	2	7
9	7	6	4	3	8	2	1	5
2	4	3	5	7	1	6	9	8
5	8	1	9	6	2	4	7	3
6	2	5	3	9	4	7	8	1
7	9	8	1	5	6	3	4	2
1	3	4	2	8	7	5	6	9

12

2	3	6	8	9	4	5	7	1
5	7	9	3	1	2	4	6	8
8	1	4	5	7	6	9	3	2
1	5	3	2	6	8	7	4	9
9	6	2	4	3	7	8	1	5
4	8	7	9	5	1	3	2	6
3	2	1	7	8	9	6	5	4
7	4	8	6	2	5	1	9	3
6	9	5	1	4	3	2	8	7

13

6	3	4	7	9	2	5	8	1
7	9	5	8	1	3	4	2	6
8	2	1	6	4	5	3	9	7
5	7	8	1	6	9	2	4	3
2	6	3	4	5	8	1	7	9
4	1	9	2	3	7	8	6	5
9	8	2	5	7	1	6	3	4
3	5	6	9	2	4	7	1	8
1	4	7	3	8	6	9	5	2

14

9	2	7	3	4	5	8	6	1
3	1	6	8	7	2	5	9	4
4	8	5	9	1	6	7	2	3
5	6	2	4	8	3	1	7	9
1	9	3	2	5	7	4	8	6
8	7	4	6	9	1	3	5	2
7	5	9	1	6	4	2	3	8
2	4	8	5	3	9	6	1	7
6	3	1	7	2	8	9	4	5

15

8	6	9	2	4	3	7	1	5
5	4	3	9	1	7	2	6	8
7	2	1	8	6	5	9	3	4
9	3	7	1	8	6	5	4	2
6	5	4	3	9	2	8	7	1
2	1	8	5	7	4	6	9	3
3	9	5	7	2	1	4	8	6
1	8	6	4	5	9	3	2	7
4	7	2	6	3	8	1	5	9

16

7	9	8	4	5	2	6	3	1
1	3	4	6	9	7	8	5	2
2	5	6	1	3	8	9	4	7
5	4	7	3	6	1	2	9	8
3	8	2	5	7	9	1	6	4
6	1	9	8	2	4	5	7	3
8	6	1	9	4	3	7	2	5
9	2	3	7	1	5	4	8	6
4	7	5	2	8	6	3	1	9

17

7	3	8	6	2	9	4	1	5
1	4	9	5	7	8	6	3	2
2	5	6	3	4	1	7	8	9
8	6	1	2	5	7	3	9	4
5	9	2	4	1	3	8	7	6
4	7	3	8	9	6	2	5	1
3	2	4	9	8	5	1	6	7
9	8	7	1	6	2	5	4	3
6	1	5	7	3	4	9	2	8

18

8	2	5	9	3	7	6	1	4
1	9	3	4	6	5	8	7	2
4	7	6	2	1	8	3	5	9
5	8	1	6	7	9	4	2	3
9	4	2	3	8	1	7	6	5
6	3	7	5	4	2	9	8	1
7	1	9	8	5	4	2	3	6
2	6	8	1	9	3	5	4	7
3	5	4	7	2	6	1	9	8

19

9	4	1	7	8	5	2	6	3
6	7	2	4	1	3	8	5	9
8	3	5	9	2	6	1	7	4
1	8	6	3	7	9	5	4	2
7	9	3	2	5	4	6	8	1
2	5	4	8	6	1	3	9	7
5	2	9	6	3	7	4	1	8
3	6	7	1	4	8	9	2	5
4	1	8	5	9	2	7	3	6

20

3	1	9	7	5	4	8	6	2
7	6	2	3	8	9	1	5	4
5	4	8	1	6	2	7	3	9
8	3	1	4	9	7	5	2	6
2	9	5	6	1	3	4	8	7
4	7	6	8	2	5	9	1	3
1	2	4	5	7	6	3	9	8
6	5	3	9	4	8	2	7	1
9	8	7	2	3	1	6	4	5

21

3	7	6	4	1	8	2	5	9
8	4	9	3	5	2	1	6	7
1	5	2	7	6	9	4	8	3
9	1	7	6	8	3	5	2	4
4	8	5	2	7	1	9	3	6
6	2	3	5	9	4	8	7	1
2	9	8	1	3	6	7	4	5
5	3	1	8	4	7	6	9	2
7	6	4	9	2	5	3	1	8

22

4	8	1	2	3	5	6	9	7
5	9	3	4	6	7	8	1	2
2	6	7	1	8	9	4	3	5
1	5	2	8	4	6	3	7	9
9	3	4	7	2	1	5	8	6
8	7	6	5	9	3	1	2	4
3	4	5	9	1	2	7	6	8
6	2	8	3	7	4	9	5	1
7	1	9	6	5	8	2	4	3

23

4	3	8	9	7	1	2	6	5
6	7	5	4	8	2	1	9	3
2	1	9	6	5	3	4	7	8
5	6	4	3	1	7	8	2	9
7	2	3	8	9	6	5	1	4
8	9	1	2	4	5	6	3	7
1	8	6	5	3	9	7	4	2
9	4	2	7	6	8	3	5	1
3	5	7	1	2	4	9	8	6

24

6	3	2	7	8	5	9	1	4
8	7	5	1	9	4	6	2	3
9	4	1	3	6	2	7	8	5
4	8	3	2	1	9	5	7	6
1	9	7	6	5	3	2	4	8
2	5	6	4	7	8	1	3	9
5	1	4	8	2	6	3	9	7
3	2	9	5	4	7	8	6	1
7	6	8	9	3	1	4	5	2

25

9	3	1	4	7	2	6	8	5
6	8	4	5	1	9	7	3	2
2	5	7	3	6	8	1	4	9
5	4	6	2	8	1	3	9	7
7	2	9	6	4	3	5	1	8
3	1	8	7	9	5	4	2	6
8	7	5	9	3	4	2	6	1
4	9	2	1	5	6	8	7	3
1	6	3	8	2	7	9	5	4

26

6	1	2	3	4	5	9	7	8
9	4	5	6	7	8	1	2	3
3	7	8	9	1	2	4	5	6
5	6	4	1	2	3	7	8	9
8	9	7	4	5	6	3	1	2
1	2	3	7	8	9	6	4	5
4	5	6	8	9	1	2	3	7
7	8	9	2	3	4	5	6	1
2	3	1	5	6	7	8	9	4

27

9	6	2	5	3	7	4	8	1
5	1	8	6	2	4	9	3	7
4	3	7	8	9	1	6	2	5
7	5	1	4	6	2	8	9	3
6	9	3	1	8	5	7	4	2
2	8	4	9	7	3	5	1	6
8	4	5	3	1	6	2	7	9
3	7	9	2	5	8	1	6	4
1	2	6	7	4	9	3	5	8

28

1	2	6	3	9	8	7	4	5
4	9	5	7	6	2	8	1	3
3	7	8	5	4	1	9	6	2
7	5	4	6	8	3	1	2	9
8	1	9	4	2	5	3	7	6
6	3	2	1	7	9	5	8	4
5	4	7	9	1	6	2	3	8
9	8	1	2	3	4	6	5	7
2	6	3	8	5	7	4	9	1

29

6	7	1	2	3	4	5	8	9
8	5	2	1	7	9	4	6	3
3	9	4	6	8	5	1	2	7
2	3	5	8	6	1	9	7	4
4	6	9	7	5	2	3	1	8
1	8	7	9	4	3	6	5	2
7	2	3	4	1	6	8	9	5
9	4	6	5	2	8	7	3	1
5	1	8	3	9	7	2	4	6

30

5	7	1	6	8	3	4	2	9
4	3	6	2	7	9	5	8	1
2	8	9	1	4	5	6	7	3
3	1	7	4	9	8	2	5	6
6	9	5	7	1	2	8	3	4
8	2	4	3	5	6	1	9	7
9	6	3	8	2	1	7	4	5
1	4	8	5	3	7	9	6	2
7	5	2	9	6	4	3	1	8

31

7	6	8	5	9	4	1	2	3
4	1	3	2	6	8	7	5	9
2	9	5	3	1	7	4	6	8
5	3	6	7	2	1	9	8	4
8	2	9	4	3	6	5	7	1
1	4	7	9	8	5	6	3	2
6	8	2	1	5	9	3	4	7
9	5	4	8	7	3	2	1	6
3	7	1	6	4	2	8	9	5

32

6	5	2	9	7	4	1	8	3
4	1	9	8	3	5	2	7	6
8	3	7	6	1	2	4	9	5
5	4	8	1	2	3	7	6	9
7	9	3	4	5	6	8	2	1
2	6	1	7	8	9	3	5	4
3	8	4	5	6	7	9	1	2
1	2	6	3	9	8	5	4	7
9	7	5	2	4	1	6	3	8

33

7	6	3	2	5	1	4	8	9
2	4	9	7	8	6	5	1	3
5	1	8	4	9	3	6	2	7
3	9	2	6	7	4	8	5	1
1	8	5	9	3	2	7	4	6
6	7	4	5	1	8	3	9	2
4	5	1	3	6	9	2	7	8
9	2	6	8	4	7	1	3	5
8	3	7	1	2	5	9	6	4

34

5	2	3	1	4	9	8	7	6
7	8	9	5	6	2	1	4	3
1	6	4	7	3	8	9	5	2
4	9	2	8	1	3	7	6	5
3	1	5	6	7	4	2	9	8
6	7	8	9	2	5	4	3	1
8	5	7	3	9	1	6	2	4
2	3	6	4	8	7	5	1	9
9	4	1	2	5	6	3	8	7

35

9	2	4	1	7	8	5	3	6
1	7	6	9	5	3	4	8	2
5	8	3	2	6	4	7	9	1
2	3	1	4	8	9	6	7	5
4	5	8	7	1	6	3	2	9
7	6	9	3	2	5	1	4	8
8	9	7	5	4	1	2	6	3
6	4	5	8	3	2	9	1	7
3	1	2	6	9	7	8	5	4

36

4	7	2	6	9	3	5	8	1
5	6	8	4	7	1	9	2	3
9	1	3	5	2	8	6	4	7
3	2	1	8	6	9	7	5	4
8	9	4	3	5	7	2	1	6
6	5	7	2	1	4	3	9	8
7	4	6	9	8	2	1	3	5
1	3	9	7	4	5	8	6	2
2	8	5	1	3	6	4	7	9

37

9	7	6	2	4	3	8	1	5
1	5	2	7	9	8	3	6	4
3	8	4	5	1	6	7	9	2
8	4	3	9	7	2	1	5	6
6	2	5	1	8	4	9	3	7
7	1	9	6	3	5	2	4	8
5	6	1	3	2	7	4	8	9
2	3	8	4	6	9	5	7	1
4	9	7	8	5	1	6	2	3

38

6	7	8	2	4	3	5	9	1
1	3	4	9	5	6	8	7	2
2	9	5	7	8	1	6	4	3
3	1	9	6	2	7	4	8	5
4	8	7	5	1	9	2	3	6
5	2	6	8	3	4	9	1	7
7	6	3	4	9	2	1	5	8
8	4	2	1	7	5	3	6	9
9	5	1	3	6	8	7	2	4

39

8	1	9	2	5	4	7	6	3
7	6	2	3	9	1	8	5	4
5	4	3	6	7	8	9	1	2
6	7	4	1	2	5	3	8	9
9	2	1	8	4	3	6	7	5
3	5	8	7	6	9	4	2	1
1	9	7	4	8	2	5	3	6
2	8	5	9	3	6	1	4	7
4	3	6	5	1	7	2	9	8

40

6	9	2	3	4	1	7	5	8
7	3	5	8	9	2	6	1	4
1	8	4	7	6	5	9	3	2
2	5	9	6	1	7	8	4	3
4	6	3	5	2	8	1	9	7
8	1	7	4	3	9	2	6	5
9	4	1	2	7	3	5	8	6
3	7	8	9	5	6	4	2	1
5	2	6	1	8	4	3	7	9

41

1	9	4	7	5	3	8	6	2
6	2	7	1	9	8	3	5	4
3	8	5	4	2	6	7	1	9
9	4	1	2	6	7	5	3	8
5	3	2	9	8	1	6	4	7
7	6	8	5	3	4	2	9	1
8	5	9	3	4	2	1	7	6
4	7	6	8	1	5	9	2	3
2	1	3	6	7	9	4	8	5

42

2	5	7	3	8	1	9	4	6
4	1	8	9	2	6	7	3	5
6	9	3	7	5	4	1	2	8
5	6	9	4	7	3	8	1	2
7	3	4	8	1	2	6	5	9
1	8	2	6	9	5	4	7	3
3	4	1	5	6	8	2	9	7
9	2	6	1	3	7	5	8	4
8	7	5	2	4	9	3	6	1

43

7	1	8	2	9	5	3	4	6
2	3	5	6	4	1	9	8	7
9	4	6	8	3	7	1	2	5
6	7	4	1	2	3	8	5	9
8	9	3	4	5	6	7	1	2
1	5	2	7	8	9	6	3	4
5	8	9	3	7	2	4	6	1
3	2	1	9	6	4	5	7	8
4	6	7	5	1	8	2	9	3

44

3	1	5	9	4	2	8	7	6
4	7	6	5	3	8	1	2	9
2	8	9	1	7	6	5	3	4
1	4	8	2	6	5	3	9	7
9	6	7	4	1	3	2	8	5
5	3	2	7	8	9	6	4	1
7	2	1	3	5	4	9	6	8
8	5	3	6	9	7	4	1	2
6	9	4	8	2	1	7	5	3

45

1	4	5	9	6	3	8	7	2
9	3	2	7	1	8	4	6	5
8	7	6	2	4	5	1	9	3
6	5	9	4	3	1	7	2	8
7	2	4	8	5	9	6	3	1
3	1	8	6	2	7	9	5	4
5	6	7	3	8	4	2	1	9
2	8	3	1	9	6	5	4	7
4	9	1	5	7	2	3	8	6

46

4	1	5	8	9	2	6	3	7
7	6	2	5	4	3	1	9	8
8	9	3	6	7	1	5	4	2
3	4	9	7	1	6	8	2	5
1	5	6	2	8	9	4	7	3
2	7	8	3	5	4	9	1	6
9	3	7	4	6	5	2	8	1
5	2	1	9	3	8	7	6	4
6	8	4	1	2	7	3	5	9

47

6	7	1	2	5	8	9	4	3
2	8	3	9	4	6	7	5	1
9	4	5	7	1	3	2	8	6
5	6	2	1	8	7	3	9	4
4	9	8	6	3	2	1	7	5
3	1	7	4	9	5	6	2	8
7	5	4	3	2	1	8	6	9
8	3	6	5	7	9	4	1	2
1	2	9	8	6	4	5	3	7

48

4	5	1	3	2	6	7	8	9
8	6	3	9	5	7	2	1	4
2	7	9	1	4	8	3	5	6
9	4	8	6	3	5	1	7	2
1	3	5	7	9	2	4	6	8
6	2	7	8	1	4	5	9	3
7	1	6	2	8	3	9	4	5
5	9	2	4	6	1	8	3	7
3	8	4	5	7	9	6	2	1

49

2	1	9	4	3	5	8	6	7
3	4	5	6	7	8	1	2	9
8	7	6	1	2	9	3	5	4
7	9	4	8	5	3	6	1	2
1	5	8	2	9	6	7	4	3
6	3	2	7	4	1	9	8	5
4	2	1	3	8	7	5	9	6
9	8	3	5	6	4	2	7	1
5	6	7	9	1	2	4	3	8

50

4	7	5	1	8	2	6	9	3
9	1	3	4	7	6	2	8	5
6	2	8	9	3	5	4	7	1
7	8	9	5	2	3	1	6	4
3	6	1	7	9	4	8	5	2
2	5	4	6	1	8	9	3	7
8	3	6	2	4	7	5	1	9
1	4	7	8	5	9	3	2	6
5	9	2	3	6	1	7	4	8

MEDIUM

51

8	2	4	3	6	1	9	5	7
5	3	1	7	9	4	2	6	8
6	9	7	2	5	8	4	3	1
3	8	9	1	4	6	5	7	2
4	6	5	8	2	7	1	9	3
1	7	2	5	3	9	8	4	6
9	5	3	6	8	2	7	1	4
7	4	8	9	1	3	6	2	5
2	1	6	4	7	5	3	8	9

52

7	3	5	4	8	6	1	9	2
1	9	2	3	5	7	6	8	4
8	6	4	2	1	9	5	3	7
4	7	8	6	3	2	9	5	1
9	1	3	5	4	8	2	7	6
2	5	6	7	9	1	8	4	3
6	4	9	8	2	3	7	1	5
3	2	1	9	7	5	4	6	8
5	8	7	1	6	4	3	2	9

53

6	1	2	3	9	4	7	8	5
8	4	7	5	2	6	9	3	1
9	5	3	8	7	1	2	4	6
1	8	5	9	6	2	3	7	4
3	2	4	7	5	8	6	1	9
7	9	6	4	1	3	8	5	2
5	6	8	2	4	7	1	9	3
2	7	9	1	3	5	4	6	8
4	3	1	6	8	9	5	2	7

54

5	1	8	7	3	2	6	9	4
2	4	3	9	8	6	1	5	7
6	9	7	1	4	5	3	2	8
7	3	1	6	9	8	5	4	2
4	6	2	3	5	7	8	1	9
8	5	9	4	2	1	7	3	6
9	7	4	5	6	3	2	8	1
3	2	6	8	1	4	9	7	5
1	8	5	2	7	9	4	6	3

55

8	3	9	5	6	2	1	4	7
5	7	4	1	9	8	6	3	2
1	2	6	7	3	4	8	9	5
9	8	1	4	7	6	5	2	3
4	5	3	2	8	1	7	6	9
2	6	7	9	5	3	4	8	1
3	9	8	6	1	7	2	5	4
6	1	2	3	4	5	9	7	8
7	4	5	8	2	9	3	1	6

56

9	7	5	4	6	8	1	3	2
6	3	1	7	9	2	4	5	8
4	8	2	1	3	5	9	7	6
5	1	4	3	2	7	6	8	9
8	6	3	9	4	1	5	2	7
2	9	7	5	8	6	3	1	4
1	5	9	2	7	4	8	6	3
3	2	6	8	5	9	7	4	1
7	4	8	6	1	3	2	9	5

57

4	7	3	5	9	2	6	1	8
1	6	2	4	8	3	7	9	5
8	9	5	7	1	6	4	3	2
5	1	8	2	6	9	3	7	4
7	2	4	1	3	5	9	8	6
6	3	9	8	4	7	2	5	1
2	5	1	3	7	4	8	6	9
3	4	6	9	5	8	1	2	7
9	8	7	6	2	1	5	4	3

58

1	9	5	6	3	2	7	8	4
8	6	2	4	7	5	9	3	1
7	3	4	8	9	1	2	6	5
9	7	3	1	5	4	8	2	6
4	8	6	9	2	3	5	1	7
5	2	1	7	6	8	4	9	3
3	4	8	5	1	9	6	7	2
2	5	7	3	8	6	1	4	9
6	1	9	2	4	7	3	5	8

59

5	7	3	2	9	8	1	6	4
8	2	9	6	4	1	7	3	5
6	4	1	5	7	3	2	9	8
3	9	5	1	2	4	6	8	7
1	8	2	3	6	7	4	5	9
4	6	7	8	5	9	3	2	1
2	1	4	9	3	5	8	7	6
7	5	6	4	8	2	9	1	3
9	3	8	7	1	6	5	4	2

60

5	4	8	2	3	9	6	1	7
2	3	6	5	1	7	4	8	9
7	1	9	6	4	8	2	5	3
4	7	5	3	6	2	1	9	8
1	9	3	4	8	5	7	6	2
6	8	2	7	9	1	5	3	4
9	5	4	1	2	3	8	7	6
3	2	1	8	7	6	9	4	5
8	6	7	9	5	4	3	2	1

61

3	7	6	1	9	8	4	5	2
1	8	4	2	7	5	6	9	3
9	2	5	3	4	6	1	7	8
5	4	3	9	6	1	2	8	7
2	9	1	4	8	7	3	6	5
8	6	7	5	3	2	9	1	4
4	5	2	8	1	9	7	3	6
6	1	8	7	2	3	5	4	9
7	3	9	6	5	4	8	2	1

62

2	1	9	3	7	4	8	5	6
5	3	6	2	8	9	7	1	4
4	7	8	1	6	5	2	9	3
1	6	2	5	9	3	4	7	8
8	4	7	6	2	1	5	3	9
9	5	3	7	4	8	1	6	2
7	2	5	4	3	6	9	8	1
6	8	4	9	1	7	3	2	5
3	9	1	8	5	2	6	4	7

63

9	5	3	4	2	1	6	8	7
4	7	8	3	5	6	1	2	9
1	2	6	7	9	8	5	4	3
3	8	4	9	1	5	2	7	6
6	9	5	2	7	3	8	1	4
2	1	7	8	6	4	9	3	5
7	6	1	5	4	2	3	9	8
5	3	9	1	8	7	4	6	2
8	4	2	6	3	9	7	5	1

64

6	8	1	4	3	2	5	7	9
5	9	2	8	7	6	3	1	4
7	4	3	5	1	9	2	6	8
2	6	9	3	4	7	8	5	1
3	5	7	6	8	1	9	4	2
8	1	4	9	2	5	6	3	7
4	7	5	2	6	8	1	9	3
1	2	6	7	9	3	4	8	5
9	3	8	1	5	4	7	2	6

65

2	6	5	9	3	1	7	4	8
9	3	8	7	6	4	1	5	2
7	4	1	2	8	5	9	6	3
5	9	4	6	2	3	8	7	1
6	8	2	1	9	7	5	3	4
3	1	7	5	4	8	2	9	6
8	5	9	3	1	6	4	2	7
4	7	3	8	5	2	6	1	9
1	2	6	4	7	9	3	8	5

66

8	5	1	2	9	4	6	7	3
6	2	4	7	3	1	5	9	8
3	7	9	5	6	8	4	1	2
4	8	7	9	1	6	3	2	5
2	6	3	4	7	5	1	8	9
9	1	5	3	8	2	7	6	4
7	4	8	6	2	3	9	5	1
5	9	2	1	4	7	8	3	6
1	3	6	8	5	9	2	4	7

67

7	6	8	5	3	2	1	4	9
2	3	1	7	4	9	8	6	5
4	5	9	8	1	6	7	2	3
6	2	5	3	9	1	4	8	7
3	1	7	4	5	8	2	9	6
9	8	4	2	6	7	5	3	1
1	4	2	6	7	3	9	5	8
8	7	6	9	2	5	3	1	4
5	9	3	1	8	4	6	7	2

68

8	4	1	3	9	7	2	5	6
7	6	9	2	8	5	4	1	3
2	3	5	1	6	4	9	7	8
1	2	3	7	4	6	5	8	9
6	5	4	9	2	8	1	3	7
9	7	8	5	3	1	6	2	4
4	1	7	6	5	3	8	9	2
3	9	6	8	1	2	7	4	5
5	8	2	4	7	9	3	6	1

69

1	3	4	8	6	5	7	9	2
9	2	6	3	7	1	8	4	5
7	8	5	2	9	4	6	1	3
5	4	3	7	1	6	2	8	9
2	9	7	4	8	3	1	5	6
6	1	8	9	5	2	4	3	7
8	5	1	6	2	9	3	7	4
4	6	9	1	3	7	5	2	8
3	7	2	5	4	8	9	6	1

70

6	8	2	3	9	5	4	7	1
7	5	1	8	4	2	6	3	9
4	3	9	7	1	6	8	5	2
5	6	4	9	2	8	7	1	3
9	2	7	1	6	3	5	4	8
8	1	3	4	5	7	9	2	6
2	9	6	5	7	1	3	8	4
3	4	5	2	8	9	1	6	7
1	7	8	6	3	4	2	9	5

71

3	7	4	6	5	9	1	8	2
6	5	1	4	8	2	7	9	3
2	8	9	7	3	1	4	6	5
1	2	5	9	4	8	6	3	7
7	9	3	1	2	6	5	4	8
8	4	6	5	7	3	2	1	9
4	1	7	8	9	5	3	2	6
5	3	8	2	6	4	9	7	1
9	6	2	3	1	7	8	5	4

72

5	3	2	6	7	1	4	8	9
9	4	1	8	3	2	6	7	5
6	8	7	4	5	9	3	1	2
2	9	3	7	4	8	1	5	6
7	6	8	5	1	3	9	2	4
1	5	4	9	2	6	7	3	8
8	7	5	3	6	4	2	9	1
3	2	6	1	9	5	8	4	7
4	1	9	2	8	7	5	6	3

73

7	6	5	4	1	3	9	8	2
9	8	1	5	6	2	7	3	4
3	2	4	7	8	9	5	6	1
6	9	3	8	7	1	2	4	5
1	7	8	2	4	5	6	9	3
5	4	2	3	9	6	1	7	8
4	3	6	1	5	7	8	2	9
8	1	9	6	2	4	3	5	7
2	5	7	9	3	8	4	1	6

74

1	4	5	3	7	2	8	9	6
6	9	3	4	8	5	7	1	2
8	2	7	6	9	1	3	5	4
7	5	9	2	6	4	1	3	8
3	1	4	8	5	7	2	6	9
2	8	6	1	3	9	5	4	7
5	6	8	7	4	3	9	2	1
4	3	1	9	2	8	6	7	5
9	7	2	5	1	6	4	8	3

75

6	1	9	5	3	8	4	7	2
5	4	8	2	7	1	9	6	3
7	3	2	6	9	4	5	8	1
4	8	3	1	2	5	7	9	6
1	7	6	8	4	9	3	2	5
9	2	5	7	6	3	1	4	8
2	5	1	4	8	7	6	3	9
8	9	7	3	1	6	2	5	4
3	6	4	9	5	2	8	1	7

76

5	8	2	6	4	7	9	1	3
4	1	7	9	3	8	5	6	2
3	9	6	5	2	1	7	8	4
7	6	3	4	8	5	2	9	1
2	4	8	3	1	9	6	5	7
9	5	1	2	7	6	4	3	8
1	2	9	8	6	4	3	7	5
8	3	5	7	9	2	1	4	6
6	7	4	1	5	3	8	2	9

77

2	7	6	3	9	5	4	1	8
5	9	4	7	8	1	6	3	2
3	1	8	4	2	6	7	5	9
6	2	7	8	5	3	9	4	1
4	8	5	2	1	9	3	7	6
9	3	1	6	7	4	2	8	5
8	6	9	1	3	7	5	2	4
7	5	2	9	4	8	1	6	3
1	4	3	5	6	2	8	9	7

78

3	5	8	2	9	1	4	6	7
6	7	9	3	5	4	8	2	1
2	4	1	8	6	7	3	9	5
1	2	4	7	8	6	9	5	3
9	6	7	1	3	5	2	4	8
5	8	3	9	4	2	7	1	6
8	3	6	5	2	9	1	7	4
7	9	5	4	1	8	6	3	2
4	1	2	6	7	3	5	8	9

79

3	5	2	7	6	9	1	8	4
7	9	4	1	2	8	6	3	5
8	1	6	5	3	4	7	2	9
4	3	1	9	8	5	2	6	7
2	7	9	6	4	1	8	5	3
6	8	5	2	7	3	4	9	1
9	2	3	8	1	7	5	4	6
1	4	8	3	5	6	9	7	2
5	6	7	4	9	2	3	1	8

80

2	3	7	5	6	4	1	8	9
9	6	4	1	8	7	2	5	3
1	8	5	2	3	9	7	4	6
6	9	3	7	5	8	4	1	2
5	2	1	4	9	3	8	6	7
4	7	8	6	1	2	9	3	5
7	4	6	8	2	5	3	9	1
3	1	2	9	4	6	5	7	8
8	5	9	3	7	1	6	2	4

81

2	5	3	9	8	6	7	1	4
1	4	8	2	5	7	9	3	6
7	9	6	3	1	4	5	2	8
4	3	1	7	2	9	8	6	5
9	8	7	6	3	5	2	4	1
5	6	2	1	4	8	3	9	7
3	1	5	8	6	2	4	7	9
8	2	9	4	7	1	6	5	3
6	7	4	5	9	3	1	8	2

82

6	5	9	1	2	4	8	3	7
7	4	8	6	9	3	1	2	5
2	1	3	7	8	5	9	4	6
4	3	2	8	5	1	6	7	9
9	6	5	3	7	2	4	1	8
8	7	1	4	6	9	2	5	3
3	8	6	2	1	7	5	9	4
1	9	4	5	3	6	7	8	2
5	2	7	9	4	8	3	6	1

83

7	3	1	5	4	2	6	9	8
9	5	6	7	1	8	2	3	4
8	4	2	6	3	9	7	1	5
6	9	3	4	8	7	1	5	2
2	7	8	1	5	6	9	4	3
5	1	4	2	9	3	8	6	7
3	6	5	8	7	1	4	2	9
1	8	9	3	2	4	5	7	6
4	2	7	9	6	5	3	8	1

84

9	1	2	4	3	5	8	7	6
6	4	5	2	8	7	1	9	3
7	8	3	6	1	9	5	4	2
3	7	4	5	2	1	9	6	8
8	9	1	3	6	4	7	2	5
2	5	6	7	9	8	3	1	4
5	6	8	1	7	2	4	3	9
4	2	7	9	5	3	6	8	1
1	3	9	8	4	6	2	5	7

85

7	3	6	5	9	1	8	4	2
1	4	8	6	2	7	3	5	9
9	2	5	3	8	4	7	6	1
6	9	4	2	1	8	5	7	3
2	8	3	9	7	5	4	1	6
5	1	7	4	6	3	9	2	8
8	6	2	7	4	9	1	3	5
4	5	9	1	3	6	2	8	7
3	7	1	8	5	2	6	9	4

86

4	9	2	3	1	7	8	6	5
1	6	8	5	4	9	7	2	3
5	7	3	6	2	8	1	9	4
2	8	4	7	5	6	9	3	1
3	5	7	4	9	1	6	8	2
9	1	6	2	8	3	4	5	7
7	4	5	9	6	2	3	1	8
6	2	1	8	3	4	5	7	9
8	3	9	1	7	5	2	4	6

87

6	1	4	5	8	2	7	9	3
8	9	3	7	4	1	2	5	6
7	5	2	6	9	3	1	8	4
9	6	1	2	7	8	4	3	5
4	8	7	9	3	5	6	2	1
3	2	5	1	6	4	9	7	8
2	3	8	4	1	9	5	6	7
5	4	6	8	2	7	3	1	9
1	7	9	3	5	6	8	4	2

88

2	1	8	3	6	9	5	4	7
4	7	6	2	1	5	8	3	9
3	5	9	7	4	8	1	6	2
1	6	2	4	8	3	9	7	5
7	8	3	5	9	2	4	1	6
9	4	5	1	7	6	3	2	8
5	2	4	9	3	7	6	8	1
6	9	1	8	2	4	7	5	3
8	3	7	6	5	1	2	9	4

89

9	6	4	1	7	5	3	2	8
2	3	1	9	4	8	5	7	6
7	8	5	6	2	3	9	4	1
3	2	6	4	8	7	1	9	5
4	7	9	3	5	1	8	6	2
5	1	8	2	9	6	7	3	4
1	9	2	8	3	4	6	5	7
8	4	7	5	6	9	2	1	3
6	5	3	7	1	2	4	8	9

90

7	2	8	5	4	6	1	3	9
9	1	4	3	8	7	2	5	6
6	3	5	9	2	1	8	4	7
3	5	1	7	6	9	4	2	8
2	8	9	4	1	3	6	7	5
4	7	6	2	5	8	3	9	1
5	6	3	8	9	4	7	1	2
8	4	2	1	7	5	9	6	3
1	9	7	6	3	2	5	8	4

91

8	7	1	2	4	5	3	9	6
6	5	4	3	9	1	2	8	7
9	2	3	6	8	7	4	5	1
4	9	7	1	6	2	5	3	8
1	3	8	4	5	9	6	7	2
5	6	2	8	7	3	1	4	9
2	4	5	7	1	8	9	6	3
3	8	6	9	2	4	7	1	5
7	1	9	5	3	6	8	2	4

92

4	8	3	2	9	5	1	7	6
6	7	5	3	1	8	9	2	4
2	1	9	6	4	7	5	8	3
1	6	8	4	7	2	3	5	9
3	4	2	5	6	9	7	1	8
5	9	7	1	8	3	6	4	2
7	3	4	9	2	1	8	6	5
8	5	6	7	3	4	2	9	1
9	2	1	8	5	6	4	3	7

93

2	5	9	6	1	8	3	4	7
4	3	1	5	7	2	9	6	8
8	7	6	9	3	4	2	1	5
9	6	2	7	4	1	8	5	3
5	4	3	2	8	9	6	7	1
1	8	7	3	6	5	4	9	2
6	9	8	1	2	7	5	3	4
3	1	4	8	5	6	7	2	9
7	2	5	4	9	3	1	8	6

94

8	7	1	6	5	3	4	9	2
9	2	5	7	4	1	6	3	8
6	4	3	9	8	2	7	5	1
4	6	9	1	3	5	8	2	7
5	1	7	8	2	6	9	4	3
3	8	2	4	9	7	5	1	6
1	9	8	3	6	4	2	7	5
2	3	6	5	7	9	1	8	4
7	5	4	2	1	8	3	6	9

95

2	4	5	7	9	1	3	8	6
8	1	7	5	6	3	4	2	9
9	3	6	8	4	2	5	1	7
3	7	1	9	2	8	6	4	5
6	5	2	4	3	7	1	9	8
4	8	9	1	5	6	2	7	3
1	9	3	6	8	4	7	5	2
5	6	4	2	7	9	8	3	1
7	2	8	3	1	5	9	6	4

96

1	5	9	6	2	7	8	3	4
6	8	2	5	3	4	9	7	1
7	3	4	1	8	9	5	2	6
2	1	3	8	4	6	7	9	5
4	6	5	7	9	3	2	1	8
9	7	8	2	1	5	6	4	3
3	2	1	9	5	8	4	6	7
5	4	6	3	7	2	1	8	9
8	9	7	4	6	1	3	5	2

97

4	6	3	2	7	1	5	9	8
9	1	5	4	8	3	6	7	2
8	2	7	5	6	9	4	1	3
1	5	9	8	2	4	7	3	6
7	4	8	3	5	6	1	2	9
2	3	6	9	1	7	8	4	5
5	8	4	7	3	2	9	6	1
6	7	2	1	9	5	3	8	4
3	9	1	6	4	8	2	5	7

98

4	8	5	6	9	2	7	1	3
1	7	6	4	8	3	9	2	5
9	2	3	7	1	5	4	6	8
3	5	1	8	7	6	2	4	9
8	6	2	3	4	9	5	7	1
7	4	9	5	2	1	3	8	6
5	3	4	2	6	8	1	9	7
2	1	8	9	5	7	6	3	4
6	9	7	1	3	4	8	5	2

99

2	7	5	8	9	1	3	6	4
6	8	1	2	4	3	9	5	7
9	3	4	6	5	7	2	1	8
3	6	8	1	7	5	4	2	9
1	4	9	3	6	2	7	8	5
5	2	7	4	8	9	6	3	1
7	1	3	5	2	4	8	9	6
4	5	6	9	3	8	1	7	2
8	9	2	7	1	6	5	4	3

100

8	5	2	7	6	9	3	1	4
3	4	9	5	8	1	7	2	6
6	1	7	2	3	4	9	8	5
9	3	1	6	7	2	4	5	8
5	6	4	8	1	3	2	7	9
7	2	8	4	9	5	1	6	3
4	8	3	1	5	7	6	9	2
2	7	6	9	4	8	5	3	1
1	9	5	3	2	6	8	4	7

101

4	1	9	2	3	7	5	8	6
6	8	5	1	9	4	3	7	2
7	2	3	5	6	8	1	4	9
3	7	1	4	2	5	9	6	8
5	9	8	6	7	3	2	1	4
2	6	4	8	1	9	7	5	3
9	5	6	7	8	2	4	3	1
8	4	2	3	5	1	6	9	7
1	3	7	9	4	6	8	2	5

102

4	9	1	5	6	3	7	8	2
8	2	3	7	9	1	5	4	6
6	5	7	2	8	4	9	1	3
7	6	4	9	3	8	2	5	1
3	1	5	4	2	7	6	9	8
9	8	2	6	1	5	3	7	4
2	4	6	8	7	9	1	3	5
5	3	9	1	4	6	8	2	7
1	7	8	3	5	2	4	6	9

103

5	9	4	6	8	3	2	7	1
7	8	6	1	5	2	9	3	4
3	2	1	9	4	7	8	6	5
4	1	3	7	9	6	5	8	2
8	6	2	5	3	1	4	9	7
9	5	7	4	2	8	6	1	3
6	4	9	3	7	5	1	2	8
2	7	5	8	1	9	3	4	6
1	3	8	2	6	4	7	5	9

104

8	1	7	5	4	3	9	6	2
4	6	9	8	7	2	3	5	1
2	3	5	1	9	6	8	7	4
3	4	2	9	8	7	5	1	6
5	8	6	4	3	1	7	2	9
7	9	1	2	6	5	4	3	8
1	2	8	7	5	4	6	9	3
9	7	3	6	2	8	1	4	5
6	5	4	3	1	9	2	8	7

105

6	9	4	8	7	1	5	3	2
1	3	2	5	9	4	6	7	8
5	8	7	3	2	6	1	9	4
3	5	6	1	8	7	4	2	9
8	2	1	4	6	9	7	5	3
4	7	9	2	5	3	8	6	1
9	4	3	7	1	5	2	8	6
7	6	8	9	4	2	3	1	5
2	1	5	6	3	8	9	4	7

106

4	9	2	7	1	5	3	8	6
6	8	5	9	3	2	4	7	1
7	1	3	6	4	8	5	2	9
5	6	7	4	2	3	1	9	8
3	4	9	8	6	1	7	5	2
1	2	8	5	7	9	6	4	3
9	3	4	2	5	6	8	1	7
2	7	1	3	8	4	9	6	5
8	5	6	1	9	7	2	3	4

107

6	3	1	5	7	9	8	2	4
7	8	4	6	2	3	1	9	5
5	9	2	8	1	4	7	6	3
2	7	3	9	5	1	4	8	6
4	5	6	2	8	7	9	3	1
8	1	9	4	3	6	5	7	2
3	6	5	7	4	8	2	1	9
9	4	7	1	6	2	3	5	8
1	2	8	3	9	5	6	4	7

108

7	5	4	3	6	2	8	9	1
1	8	3	9	7	5	6	2	4
6	2	9	4	8	1	7	3	5
9	1	7	8	5	4	2	6	3
2	6	8	1	3	7	5	4	9
3	4	5	6	2	9	1	8	7
8	7	6	5	4	3	9	1	2
5	3	1	2	9	8	4	7	6
4	9	2	7	1	6	3	5	8

109

6	7	9	2	5	1	8	3	4
5	1	2	8	3	4	7	6	9
4	8	3	6	9	7	5	1	2
1	2	5	3	7	8	9	4	6
9	3	7	4	6	5	2	8	1
8	6	4	1	2	9	3	5	7
3	4	1	7	8	2	6	9	5
2	9	6	5	4	3	1	7	8
7	5	8	9	1	6	4	2	3

110

9	6	7	4	8	2	1	3	5
5	4	8	3	9	1	6	2	7
3	2	1	6	7	5	4	8	9
7	8	6	5	4	3	9	1	2
1	3	4	7	2	9	5	6	8
2	9	5	1	6	8	7	4	3
8	1	3	9	5	4	2	7	6
6	5	2	8	1	7	3	9	4
4	7	9	2	3	6	8	5	1

111

5	1	7	9	3	8	2	4	6
4	6	3	5	2	1	7	9	8
8	2	9	4	7	6	3	1	5
1	9	6	3	4	5	8	2	7
2	5	8	6	1	7	9	3	4
3	7	4	2	8	9	6	5	1
9	3	5	8	6	4	1	7	2
7	8	2	1	5	3	4	6	9
6	4	1	7	9	2	5	8	3

112

5	9	2	4	7	1	3	6	8
6	8	7	3	5	9	1	4	2
3	1	4	8	2	6	5	9	7
4	3	8	6	9	2	7	1	5
2	7	6	5	1	4	8	3	9
9	5	1	7	8	3	4	2	6
8	6	9	1	3	7	2	5	4
7	4	3	2	6	5	9	8	1
1	2	5	9	4	8	6	7	3

113

3	2	8	6	9	7	1	4	5
5	7	4	2	1	3	6	8	9
1	6	9	8	5	4	3	7	2
8	5	7	3	4	6	2	9	1
9	4	6	1	2	5	7	3	8
2	1	3	7	8	9	5	6	4
7	8	5	9	3	2	4	1	6
4	3	1	5	6	8	9	2	7
6	9	2	4	7	1	8	5	3

114

1	9	5	3	6	2	8	7	4
8	3	7	4	1	9	5	6	2
6	2	4	7	5	8	1	3	9
3	8	6	1	4	7	2	9	5
7	5	9	2	8	6	4	1	3
2	4	1	9	3	5	7	8	6
9	7	3	5	2	1	6	4	8
4	6	2	8	7	3	9	5	1
5	1	8	6	9	4	3	2	7

115

9	7	2	8	3	6	4	5	1
1	4	8	2	5	9	3	6	7
6	3	5	1	7	4	2	8	9
7	2	3	9	6	5	1	4	8
5	1	6	3	4	8	7	9	2
4	8	9	7	1	2	5	3	6
3	5	7	6	8	1	9	2	4
8	9	1	4	2	3	6	7	5
2	6	4	5	9	7	8	1	3

116

9	1	8	2	3	4	7	6	5
2	7	5	9	6	1	8	3	4
6	4	3	8	7	5	1	2	9
4	5	6	1	9	3	2	8	7
8	9	2	6	4	7	3	5	1
7	3	1	5	2	8	9	4	6
5	8	4	3	1	9	6	7	2
1	6	7	4	8	2	5	9	3
3	2	9	7	5	6	4	1	8

117

6	9	8	1	4	3	5	2	7
2	3	4	7	5	9	1	6	8
5	1	7	2	6	8	9	4	3
3	6	2	8	7	1	4	5	9
7	4	9	5	2	6	8	3	1
1	8	5	3	9	4	2	7	6
9	2	6	4	8	7	3	1	5
8	5	3	6	1	2	7	9	4
4	7	1	9	3	5	6	8	2

118

9	2	8	7	4	1	6	5	3
3	6	1	8	5	9	2	7	4
4	5	7	6	2	3	9	8	1
8	1	3	9	6	4	7	2	5
6	4	5	1	7	2	8	3	9
7	9	2	3	8	5	1	4	6
1	8	4	5	9	7	3	6	2
5	7	9	2	3	6	4	1	8
2	3	6	4	1	8	5	9	7

119

4	7	3	8	9	2	5	1	6
9	5	6	1	4	3	7	2	8
8	1	2	7	6	5	4	3	9
5	6	1	3	8	7	2	9	4
7	8	9	6	2	4	1	5	3
3	2	4	5	1	9	8	6	7
2	3	5	9	7	8	6	4	1
1	4	7	2	3	6	9	8	5
6	9	8	4	5	1	3	7	2

120

7	5	4	2	8	6	9	1	3
6	2	9	3	5	1	7	8	4
1	8	3	7	9	4	5	2	6
3	4	5	1	6	8	2	9	7
8	6	1	9	7	2	3	4	5
9	7	2	5	4	3	8	6	1
4	3	7	6	2	9	1	5	8
5	9	6	8	1	7	4	3	2
2	1	8	4	3	5	6	7	9

121

1	3	6	8	4	9	5	2	7
8	4	9	7	2	5	3	6	1
5	7	2	3	6	1	8	9	4
3	6	8	9	5	4	1	7	2
9	2	4	1	7	3	6	8	5
7	1	5	6	8	2	9	4	3
4	9	7	5	3	8	2	1	6
2	5	1	4	9	6	7	3	8
6	8	3	2	1	7	4	5	9

122

2	8	3	7	5	4	1	9	6
6	5	9	3	1	8	2	7	4
7	1	4	2	6	9	3	8	5
1	9	7	5	3	2	6	4	8
5	6	8	4	7	1	9	2	3
4	3	2	8	9	6	5	1	7
9	4	5	1	8	3	7	6	2
3	2	1	6	4	7	8	5	9
8	7	6	9	2	5	4	3	1

123

9	4	7	1	3	6	8	5	2
2	8	3	5	7	4	6	9	1
5	1	6	2	9	8	4	3	7
6	5	4	8	2	3	7	1	9
8	3	9	6	1	7	5	2	4
1	7	2	4	5	9	3	8	6
7	2	5	3	6	1	9	4	8
3	6	8	9	4	2	1	7	5
4	9	1	7	8	5	2	6	3

124

9	1	8	7	2	4	5	6	3
2	4	3	8	5	6	1	9	7
6	5	7	1	3	9	2	4	8
4	3	6	5	9	8	7	2	1
7	2	9	6	1	3	4	8	5
5	8	1	2	4	7	9	3	6
8	7	4	9	6	5	3	1	2
1	9	5	3	8	2	6	7	4
3	6	2	4	7	1	8	5	9

125

6	1	4	9	5	3	7	8	2
2	8	7	1	4	6	5	3	9
5	3	9	2	8	7	4	1	6
4	7	6	8	3	1	2	9	5
3	2	1	5	9	4	8	6	7
8	9	5	7	6	2	3	4	1
7	6	2	3	1	8	9	5	4
1	5	3	4	2	9	6	7	8
9	4	8	6	7	5	1	2	3

126

8	6	9	1	5	2	3	4	7
7	2	1	3	6	4	9	8	5
5	3	4	7	9	8	6	2	1
4	8	3	5	2	6	7	1	9
1	5	2	8	7	9	4	6	3
6	9	7	4	3	1	2	5	8
3	7	6	2	8	5	1	9	4
9	1	5	6	4	7	8	3	2
2	4	8	9	1	3	5	7	6

127

9	4	3	8	2	6	1	5	7
5	6	8	7	9	1	3	2	4
7	1	2	3	4	5	9	6	8
6	3	5	1	8	9	7	4	2
8	9	1	2	7	4	6	3	5
4	2	7	5	6	3	8	9	1
1	5	4	6	3	8	2	7	9
3	7	9	4	1	2	5	8	6
2	8	6	9	5	7	4	1	3

128

8	2	6	7	9	3	1	5	4
9	7	5	8	4	1	2	6	3
1	4	3	6	2	5	9	7	8
2	3	8	9	5	7	6	4	1
5	6	7	4	1	2	8	3	9
4	9	1	3	8	6	7	2	5
3	8	4	2	7	9	5	1	6
7	1	9	5	6	4	3	8	2
6	5	2	1	3	8	4	9	7

129

3	5	8	2	4	1	6	7	9
2	7	9	6	5	3	8	1	4
6	4	1	8	7	9	5	3	2
4	9	6	1	2	5	3	8	7
1	8	3	4	9	7	2	5	6
5	2	7	3	6	8	9	4	1
7	6	2	5	8	4	1	9	3
8	1	4	9	3	2	7	6	5
9	3	5	7	1	6	4	2	8

130

7	9	5	6	8	4	1	3	2
3	4	2	5	1	9	8	6	7
1	6	8	7	2	3	5	4	9
5	1	6	9	4	8	7	2	3
8	2	7	3	5	6	4	9	1
4	3	9	1	7	2	6	5	8
6	5	3	8	9	7	2	1	4
2	8	1	4	3	5	9	7	6
9	7	4	2	6	1	3	8	5

131

5	6	7	9	8	4	2	3	1
3	2	8	1	5	7	6	9	4
9	1	4	2	6	3	8	7	5
4	7	5	6	9	2	1	8	3
2	8	3	7	4	1	9	5	6
1	9	6	5	3	8	4	2	7
6	3	2	8	1	5	7	4	9
8	4	1	3	7	9	5	6	2
7	5	9	4	2	6	3	1	8

132

8	3	5	7	1	6	2	4	9
9	4	6	5	2	8	1	7	3
2	7	1	4	3	9	8	5	6
3	8	2	1	9	7	5	6	4
1	6	7	8	5	4	3	9	2
4	5	9	2	6	3	7	1	8
7	1	3	6	4	2	9	8	5
6	9	8	3	7	5	4	2	1
5	2	4	9	8	1	6	3	7

133

7	1	9	6	4	3	2	5	8
3	2	6	5	8	7	9	4	1
4	8	5	9	1	2	3	7	6
1	6	7	4	5	9	8	3	2
2	4	3	1	7	8	5	6	9
5	9	8	3	2	6	4	1	7
9	3	4	8	6	1	7	2	5
6	5	2	7	9	4	1	8	3
8	7	1	2	3	5	6	9	4

134

9	1	8	4	3	2	5	6	7
2	6	7	5	1	8	4	9	3
5	3	4	9	7	6	2	8	1
4	5	1	3	9	7	8	2	6
6	7	2	1	8	4	3	5	9
3	8	9	2	6	5	7	1	4
1	4	6	8	2	3	9	7	5
8	9	5	7	4	1	6	3	2
7	2	3	6	5	9	1	4	8

135

2	7	3	1	5	8	9	4	6
1	9	8	7	6	4	3	5	2
4	6	5	9	2	3	7	8	1
6	5	4	3	9	2	8	1	7
7	2	1	8	4	6	5	3	9
3	8	9	5	1	7	2	6	4
9	1	2	6	8	5	4	7	3
5	3	6	4	7	9	1	2	8
8	4	7	2	3	1	6	9	5

136

7	1	2	8	5	6	9	3	4
4	3	8	2	7	9	6	1	5
6	9	5	3	4	1	7	8	2
3	5	7	1	6	2	4	9	8
1	2	6	9	8	4	3	5	7
8	4	9	5	3	7	1	2	6
5	8	4	7	1	3	2	6	9
9	7	3	6	2	8	5	4	1
2	6	1	4	9	5	8	7	3

137

9	7	1	4	6	5	8	3	2
2	5	3	8	7	9	6	1	4
8	4	6	2	3	1	9	7	5
7	3	8	6	9	4	5	2	1
1	6	2	7	5	8	3	4	9
4	9	5	3	1	2	7	6	8
5	1	7	9	4	6	2	8	3
3	2	4	5	8	7	1	9	6
6	8	9	1	2	3	4	5	7

138

8	5	9	6	3	4	1	7	2
2	1	4	9	5	7	3	6	8
3	7	6	8	1	2	9	4	5
4	6	7	2	9	3	8	5	1
9	8	3	5	6	1	7	2	4
1	2	5	7	4	8	6	9	3
5	3	8	4	7	6	2	1	9
6	4	2	1	8	9	5	3	7
7	9	1	3	2	5	4	8	6

139

4	5	9	8	2	3	7	6	1
7	1	2	9	6	4	8	5	3
8	3	6	1	7	5	9	2	4
2	9	7	6	4	8	3	1	5
5	6	3	7	1	9	4	8	2
1	8	4	5	3	2	6	9	7
6	2	1	3	9	7	5	4	8
3	4	8	2	5	6	1	7	9
9	7	5	4	8	1	2	3	6

140

3	2	8	4	7	6	9	1	5
9	1	6	3	8	5	4	2	7
5	7	4	2	1	9	3	6	8
2	3	7	6	9	1	5	8	4
6	8	1	5	4	3	2	7	9
4	9	5	7	2	8	1	3	6
1	6	9	8	3	4	7	5	2
8	4	2	1	5	7	6	9	3
7	5	3	9	6	2	8	4	1

141

5	2	3	1	6	8	7	4	9
8	4	9	7	5	2	6	3	1
7	1	6	9	4	3	5	8	2
6	3	2	5	8	4	9	1	7
1	9	5	6	3	7	8	2	4
4	7	8	2	9	1	3	5	6
3	5	7	4	2	9	1	6	8
2	6	1	8	7	5	4	9	3
9	8	4	3	1	6	2	7	5

142

4	5	8	7	1	9	6	3	2
2	9	3	4	8	6	5	7	1
6	1	7	3	2	5	8	9	4
5	3	9	8	6	4	1	2	7
8	6	4	2	7	1	3	5	9
7	2	1	5	9	3	4	6	8
1	8	6	9	5	7	2	4	3
3	7	5	1	4	2	9	8	6
9	4	2	6	3	8	7	1	5

143

5	3	7	9	6	8	4	1	2
1	6	8	2	4	5	7	3	9
4	2	9	3	1	7	5	8	6
3	7	6	4	5	1	9	2	8
2	1	5	8	7	9	3	6	4
8	9	4	6	3	2	1	5	7
6	5	2	1	9	4	8	7	3
7	4	3	5	8	6	2	9	1
9	8	1	7	2	3	6	4	5

144

4	2	1	5	8	7	6	9	3
6	3	5	9	1	2	4	8	7
8	9	7	3	6	4	1	5	2
3	6	9	7	5	1	2	4	8
7	1	2	8	4	3	5	6	9
5	8	4	2	9	6	7	3	1
1	4	8	6	2	9	3	7	5
9	7	6	1	3	5	8	2	4
2	5	3	4	7	8	9	1	6

145

5	8	9	6	7	1	3	4	2
3	2	7	4	5	9	8	1	6
6	1	4	2	8	3	5	9	7
4	6	5	9	2	8	1	7	3
2	7	1	3	6	5	9	8	4
8	9	3	1	4	7	6	2	5
1	5	8	7	3	2	4	6	9
9	4	2	5	1	6	7	3	8
7	3	6	8	9	4	2	5	1

146

2	4	8	5	9	3	6	7	1
1	6	5	8	2	7	9	3	4
3	9	7	6	4	1	8	5	2
6	8	2	7	3	4	5	1	9
9	5	1	2	8	6	7	4	3
4	7	3	1	5	9	2	6	8
7	3	6	9	1	8	4	2	5
5	1	9	4	7	2	3	8	6
8	2	4	3	6	5	1	9	7

147

5	2	4	3	9	8	1	7	6
7	9	1	2	6	4	5	3	8
8	3	6	5	1	7	4	9	2
6	4	5	8	7	3	9	2	1
1	8	3	9	5	2	6	4	7
2	7	9	6	4	1	8	5	3
4	5	7	1	2	6	3	8	9
9	6	8	7	3	5	2	1	4
3	1	2	4	8	9	7	6	5

148

9	6	8	1	5	4	7	3	2
1	7	4	3	9	2	6	8	5
5	3	2	8	6	7	1	9	4
8	9	6	7	2	1	5	4	3
3	4	5	9	8	6	2	7	1
7	2	1	5	4	3	9	6	8
2	8	7	4	1	9	3	5	6
6	5	3	2	7	8	4	1	9
4	1	9	6	3	5	8	2	7

149

6	8	9	7	5	4	1	3	2
3	7	4	1	9	2	6	5	8
5	1	2	3	6	8	4	9	7
9	5	8	2	1	6	3	7	4
7	4	3	9	8	5	2	6	1
1	2	6	4	7	3	5	8	9
8	3	1	6	2	9	7	4	5
2	6	5	8	4	7	9	1	3
4	9	7	5	3	1	8	2	6

150

2	9	4	5	1	3	6	8	7
3	1	7	2	8	6	9	5	4
5	6	8	9	7	4	2	1	3
6	5	2	1	4	9	3	7	8
8	3	1	7	6	5	4	2	9
4	7	9	3	2	8	1	6	5
9	8	3	6	5	2	7	4	1
1	4	6	8	3	7	5	9	2
7	2	5	4	9	1	8	3	6

151

8	6	1	3	4	5	9	2	7
3	7	4	9	6	2	5	1	8
9	2	5	8	1	7	3	4	6
6	4	3	7	2	9	1	8	5
2	9	7	5	8	1	6	3	4
5	1	8	6	3	4	2	7	9
4	5	9	1	7	3	8	6	2
7	3	6	2	5	8	4	9	1
1	8	2	4	9	6	7	5	3

152

9	6	5	8	4	3	2	1	7
8	2	7	6	1	5	4	9	3
4	1	3	2	9	7	5	8	6
5	7	9	4	3	1	6	2	8
3	4	2	9	6	8	7	5	1
1	8	6	7	5	2	3	4	9
7	9	1	5	2	6	8	3	4
6	5	4	3	8	9	1	7	2
2	3	8	1	7	4	9	6	5

153

1	7	3	5	2	4	8	9	6
9	4	2	8	6	3	1	7	5
6	8	5	1	9	7	3	2	4
2	5	7	4	3	1	6	8	9
3	9	4	6	5	8	2	1	7
8	1	6	2	7	9	4	5	3
7	6	1	3	8	5	9	4	2
4	2	9	7	1	6	5	3	8
5	3	8	9	4	2	7	6	1

154

2	5	6	7	8	1	3	9	4
9	4	1	5	3	6	7	2	8
3	8	7	2	9	4	5	6	1
8	7	3	4	2	5	9	1	6
5	2	4	1	6	9	8	7	3
6	1	9	3	7	8	2	4	5
1	9	5	8	4	7	6	3	2
4	6	2	9	5	3	1	8	7
7	3	8	6	1	2	4	5	9

155

8	7	1	9	5	6	2	4	3
3	4	9	2	7	1	6	8	5
2	6	5	8	3	4	1	7	9
6	2	4	1	8	5	3	9	7
7	5	8	6	9	3	4	1	2
9	1	3	4	2	7	5	6	8
1	8	7	5	6	2	9	3	4
4	3	2	7	1	9	8	5	6
5	9	6	3	4	8	7	2	1

156

2	7	8	3	4	1	9	5	6
3	6	4	5	7	9	2	8	1
1	5	9	6	2	8	7	4	3
7	8	1	2	5	4	6	3	9
9	4	6	8	1	3	5	7	2
5	2	3	7	9	6	4	1	8
8	9	2	4	3	5	1	6	7
4	3	7	1	6	2	8	9	5
6	1	5	9	8	7	3	2	4

157

5	2	3	8	4	6	1	9	7
9	4	8	7	5	1	6	2	3
1	6	7	2	9	3	8	5	4
7	9	2	5	6	8	4	3	1
6	3	4	9	1	7	5	8	2
8	5	1	4	3	2	7	6	9
2	8	5	1	7	9	3	4	6
3	7	9	6	8	4	2	1	5
4	1	6	3	2	5	9	7	8

158

1	4	9	7	5	8	6	2	3
8	3	2	4	6	9	7	1	5
6	7	5	1	3	2	9	4	8
3	9	6	2	7	1	8	5	4
2	8	7	5	9	4	1	3	6
5	1	4	3	8	6	2	9	7
7	2	1	8	4	5	3	6	9
4	6	3	9	1	7	5	8	2
9	5	8	6	2	3	4	7	1

159

7	4	8	5	2	1	6	9	3
5	3	1	9	6	4	7	2	8
6	2	9	8	3	7	1	5	4
1	9	6	2	5	3	8	4	7
2	8	7	4	9	6	5	3	1
4	5	3	7	1	8	2	6	9
9	6	4	1	8	2	3	7	5
3	1	5	6	7	9	4	8	2
8	7	2	3	4	5	9	1	6

160

9	4	1	8	2	7	6	3	5
7	6	5	9	3	1	2	8	4
3	2	8	4	6	5	7	9	1
1	3	9	7	4	6	8	5	2
4	8	6	2	5	3	1	7	9
5	7	2	1	8	9	3	4	6
6	1	4	5	7	8	9	2	3
8	5	3	6	9	2	4	1	7
2	9	7	3	1	4	5	6	8

161

6	3	9	5	7	4	1	8	2
2	5	1	3	8	6	4	9	7
8	4	7	9	2	1	6	3	5
1	6	3	2	5	8	7	4	9
9	8	5	1	4	7	2	6	3
7	2	4	6	3	9	5	1	8
4	9	8	7	6	2	3	5	1
5	7	6	8	1	3	9	2	4
3	1	2	4	9	5	8	7	6

162

1	9	2	6	3	5	7	8	4
8	4	3	7	9	1	2	6	5
6	7	5	2	4	8	3	9	1
5	2	7	8	1	6	9	4	3
3	1	4	5	7	9	6	2	8
9	8	6	3	2	4	1	5	7
4	6	1	9	5	3	8	7	2
2	5	9	1	8	7	4	3	6
7	3	8	4	6	2	5	1	9

163

8	9	7	4	3	1	6	2	5
3	4	2	8	6	5	7	1	9
1	6	5	9	2	7	3	4	8
6	3	8	2	1	4	9	5	7
9	7	4	6	5	8	2	3	1
5	2	1	7	9	3	4	8	6
2	8	3	1	7	6	5	9	4
4	5	6	3	8	9	1	7	2
7	1	9	5	4	2	8	6	3

164

2	8	9	6	3	1	5	4	7
1	7	5	2	4	9	8	6	3
6	4	3	5	8	7	9	1	2
8	1	7	3	2	4	6	5	9
3	9	2	1	5	6	7	8	4
5	6	4	7	9	8	2	3	1
9	2	1	4	6	5	3	7	8
7	3	6	8	1	2	4	9	5
4	5	8	9	7	3	1	2	6

165

2	1	4	3	7	5	6	8	9
8	6	3	2	1	9	4	7	5
5	9	7	4	6	8	2	1	3
9	3	8	1	5	4	7	2	6
4	2	1	6	9	7	3	5	8
6	7	5	8	2	3	9	4	1
3	5	6	7	4	1	8	9	2
7	8	9	5	3	2	1	6	4
1	4	2	9	8	6	5	3	7

166

9	6	4	3	7	1	5	2	8
2	3	8	4	6	5	7	1	9
5	7	1	9	2	8	4	3	6
6	4	9	2	8	3	1	7	5
8	2	5	7	1	4	9	6	3
3	1	7	6	5	9	2	8	4
7	9	3	1	4	6	8	5	2
1	8	6	5	9	2	3	4	7
4	5	2	8	3	7	6	9	1

167

1	2	8	9	6	4	7	3	5
4	5	9	3	7	1	2	8	6
6	3	7	2	5	8	4	9	1
5	6	2	7	1	3	9	4	8
7	9	1	8	4	2	5	6	3
3	8	4	5	9	6	1	2	7
8	4	5	1	3	9	6	7	2
2	7	6	4	8	5	3	1	9
9	1	3	6	2	7	8	5	4

168

4	7	5	6	9	3	2	8	1
2	3	9	8	4	1	7	5	6
1	8	6	5	2	7	4	9	3
8	5	4	7	3	2	6	1	9
9	1	2	4	6	8	5	3	7
3	6	7	1	5	9	8	4	2
5	4	3	9	7	6	1	2	8
7	2	8	3	1	5	9	6	4
6	9	1	2	8	4	3	7	5

169

8	9	1	4	2	7	3	6	5
5	4	6	3	8	9	2	7	1
7	3	2	6	5	1	4	9	8
4	6	7	2	9	8	1	5	3
2	5	3	7	1	4	6	8	9
1	8	9	5	3	6	7	2	4
6	1	5	9	4	2	8	3	7
9	7	8	1	6	3	5	4	2
3	2	4	8	7	5	9	1	6

170

3	9	7	1	4	6	2	8	5
4	6	2	5	9	8	1	7	3
1	8	5	7	3	2	9	4	6
8	1	4	9	7	3	5	6	2
5	2	3	8	6	4	7	1	9
6	7	9	2	1	5	4	3	8
9	3	8	4	2	7	6	5	1
2	4	6	3	5	1	8	9	7
7	5	1	6	8	9	3	2	4

171

6	4	1	2	8	7	3	9	5
7	5	2	3	9	1	6	4	8
8	9	3	4	5	6	7	2	1
5	3	7	6	1	9	2	8	4
1	2	8	7	4	5	9	6	3
9	6	4	8	3	2	5	1	7
4	8	5	9	6	3	1	7	2
2	1	6	5	7	4	8	3	9
3	7	9	1	2	8	4	5	6

172

4	8	7	9	2	3	6	5	1
9	2	1	6	5	4	3	7	8
6	3	5	7	1	8	9	4	2
5	6	3	2	4	7	8	1	9
7	9	8	1	3	6	4	2	5
2	1	4	5	8	9	7	3	6
8	7	2	4	6	5	1	9	3
1	4	6	3	9	2	5	8	7
3	5	9	8	7	1	2	6	4

173

8	2	9	7	6	3	5	4	1
3	7	6	4	1	5	9	8	2
5	1	4	2	8	9	6	7	3
2	6	3	1	4	8	7	9	5
7	4	5	3	9	2	8	1	6
9	8	1	6	5	7	2	3	4
4	5	2	9	7	1	3	6	8
1	3	7	8	2	6	4	5	9
6	9	8	5	3	4	1	2	7

174

5	1	9	6	2	3	7	8	4
4	3	8	1	5	7	2	9	6
7	6	2	4	9	8	1	3	5
9	8	1	5	7	6	3	4	2
2	4	5	8	3	1	9	6	7
3	7	6	2	4	9	8	5	1
1	9	4	7	8	5	6	2	3
6	5	3	9	1	2	4	7	8
8	2	7	3	6	4	5	1	9

175

5	3	1	2	8	7	6	4	9
6	2	4	9	1	5	7	3	8
8	9	7	4	3	6	1	5	2
4	6	5	7	9	3	8	2	1
2	1	3	6	4	8	9	7	5
7	8	9	5	2	1	3	6	4
9	7	6	1	5	2	4	8	3
1	5	8	3	6	4	2	9	7
3	4	2	8	7	9	5	1	6

176

5	9	6	8	7	4	1	2	3
8	1	2	3	5	6	4	9	7
7	4	3	2	9	1	5	8	6
9	5	4	6	8	7	2	3	1
1	2	7	9	3	5	8	6	4
6	3	8	1	4	2	9	7	5
3	6	5	4	2	8	7	1	9
4	8	9	7	1	3	6	5	2
2	7	1	5	6	9	3	4	8

177

2	1	8	3	9	5	4	7	6
5	4	6	8	7	1	3	2	9
9	3	7	4	2	6	8	1	5
1	6	3	9	8	7	5	4	2
4	8	2	5	1	3	9	6	7
7	9	5	6	4	2	1	3	8
6	5	1	7	3	8	2	9	4
8	2	4	1	6	9	7	5	3
3	7	9	2	5	4	6	8	1

178

6	7	1	2	9	5	8	4	3
4	5	3	1	6	8	7	2	9
2	8	9	4	3	7	1	6	5
7	2	4	8	1	9	5	3	6
8	3	5	6	4	2	9	7	1
1	9	6	5	7	3	2	8	4
5	4	2	9	8	6	3	1	7
3	1	8	7	5	4	6	9	2
9	6	7	3	2	1	4	5	8

179

1	6	5	2	8	9	4	3	7
8	3	7	4	1	6	5	2	9
2	9	4	3	7	5	1	6	8
9	5	2	7	4	3	8	1	6
6	4	8	9	2	1	3	7	5
3	7	1	6	5	8	9	4	2
7	1	3	5	9	2	6	8	4
4	8	9	1	6	7	2	5	3
5	2	6	8	3	4	7	9	1

180

8	9	4	5	1	6	3	2	7
5	7	2	3	9	8	4	1	6
6	3	1	7	2	4	9	5	8
4	6	8	2	3	5	1	7	9
2	1	7	8	6	9	5	4	3
9	5	3	4	7	1	6	8	2
3	2	6	1	5	7	8	9	4
1	4	9	6	8	2	7	3	5
7	8	5	9	4	3	2	6	1

181

8	9	4	6	1	3	7	2	5
1	7	6	5	2	9	8	3	4
5	2	3	8	4	7	9	6	1
7	8	5	3	6	4	1	9	2
2	6	1	9	7	5	4	8	3
4	3	9	1	8	2	6	5	7
6	5	8	4	3	1	2	7	9
9	1	7	2	5	6	3	4	8
3	4	2	7	9	8	5	1	6

182

8	6	2	5	1	3	7	4	9
5	7	4	9	8	6	1	2	3
9	1	3	2	7	4	5	8	6
3	8	1	4	6	5	9	7	2
4	2	7	8	3	9	6	1	5
6	5	9	1	2	7	4	3	8
1	3	6	7	9	8	2	5	4
2	9	5	3	4	1	8	6	7
7	4	8	6	5	2	3	9	1

183

2	9	4	1	3	5	6	8	7
5	8	6	7	4	9	3	2	1
3	7	1	2	6	8	5	9	4
7	6	2	8	5	1	9	4	3
9	4	3	6	7	2	8	1	5
8	1	5	4	9	3	7	6	2
1	5	9	3	2	6	4	7	8
6	2	7	5	8	4	1	3	9
4	3	8	9	1	7	2	5	6

184

1	6	9	4	5	2	8	3	7
4	5	3	8	6	7	2	9	1
2	8	7	1	9	3	4	5	6
9	2	8	7	4	6	3	1	5
7	4	5	3	1	8	6	2	9
3	1	6	5	2	9	7	4	8
8	9	1	2	7	4	5	6	3
6	3	4	9	8	5	1	7	2
5	7	2	6	3	1	9	8	4

185

8	2	9	6	5	4	7	3	1
5	6	7	3	1	8	4	9	2
4	1	3	7	2	9	8	5	6
1	7	5	8	6	3	9	2	4
3	8	4	5	9	2	1	6	7
2	9	6	4	7	1	3	8	5
7	3	8	2	4	6	5	1	9
9	4	2	1	8	5	6	7	3
6	5	1	9	3	7	2	4	8

186

4	1	6	5	2	8	9	3	7
2	8	9	6	7	3	4	5	1
3	5	7	4	1	9	2	8	6
1	7	4	9	8	6	3	2	5
8	9	2	3	5	1	6	7	4
6	3	5	2	4	7	8	1	9
5	6	8	7	3	4	1	9	2
9	2	3	1	6	5	7	4	8
7	4	1	8	9	2	5	6	3

187

8	3	9	7	2	5	6	4	1
5	6	7	4	3	1	9	2	8
2	4	1	6	9	8	7	3	5
3	2	6	5	1	4	8	9	7
4	1	5	9	8	7	3	6	2
9	7	8	3	6	2	5	1	4
6	8	2	1	5	9	4	7	3
1	9	4	8	7	3	2	5	6
7	5	3	2	4	6	1	8	9

188

9	3	1	6	4	2	8	5	7
4	6	8	3	5	7	9	1	2
7	5	2	1	8	9	3	4	6
3	4	5	9	2	8	7	6	1
1	9	7	4	6	3	5	2	8
8	2	6	7	1	5	4	3	9
6	1	9	8	3	4	2	7	5
2	8	4	5	7	6	1	9	3
5	7	3	2	9	1	6	8	4

189

8	4	6	1	5	7	2	9	3
1	5	3	9	2	6	4	8	7
2	9	7	8	4	3	1	6	5
4	2	5	3	7	8	6	1	9
3	1	9	4	6	2	5	7	8
6	7	8	5	9	1	3	4	2
9	8	2	6	1	5	7	3	4
7	6	4	2	3	9	8	5	1
5	3	1	7	8	4	9	2	6

190

4	7	2	1	5	8	6	9	3
9	5	1	3	6	4	2	8	7
8	3	6	2	9	7	5	1	4
6	9	7	5	8	2	3	4	1
3	8	5	7	4	1	9	2	6
1	2	4	9	3	6	7	5	8
7	6	8	4	2	5	1	3	9
5	1	9	8	7	3	4	6	2
2	4	3	6	1	9	8	7	5

191

2	1	4	3	7	8	6	9	5
6	7	9	5	4	2	8	3	1
3	5	8	6	9	1	4	2	7
5	8	2	1	3	6	9	7	4
1	9	3	7	8	4	2	5	6
4	6	7	9	2	5	3	1	8
7	2	1	4	6	9	5	8	3
8	4	5	2	1	3	7	6	9
9	3	6	8	5	7	1	4	2

192

4	1	9	6	5	8	7	2	3
6	3	5	9	2	7	8	4	1
7	2	8	3	4	1	5	9	6
5	4	1	2	7	9	3	6	8
8	7	3	4	6	5	2	1	9
2	9	6	1	8	3	4	7	5
3	6	7	8	9	4	1	5	2
9	8	4	5	1	2	6	3	7
1	5	2	7	3	6	9	8	4

193

1	5	8	9	3	4	7	6	2
2	3	6	5	8	7	1	9	4
9	7	4	1	2	6	8	5	3
6	9	7	3	1	8	2	4	5
3	8	2	4	7	5	6	1	9
5	4	1	2	6	9	3	7	8
7	6	9	8	4	2	5	3	1
8	1	5	7	9	3	4	2	6
4	2	3	6	5	1	9	8	7

194

6	4	7	3	9	1	8	5	2
9	8	3	6	2	5	7	4	1
2	1	5	8	4	7	3	9	6
1	2	8	4	7	3	5	6	9
4	5	6	2	8	9	1	3	7
7	3	9	5	1	6	4	2	8
5	6	2	1	3	8	9	7	4
8	7	4	9	5	2	6	1	3
3	9	1	7	6	4	2	8	5

195

4	6	2	1	7	3	5	8	9
5	9	3	6	2	8	4	1	7
1	7	8	9	5	4	2	6	3
2	8	5	4	9	7	1	3	6
6	3	7	5	1	2	9	4	8
9	1	4	3	8	6	7	5	2
8	5	6	2	4	9	3	7	1
7	2	1	8	3	5	6	9	4
3	4	9	7	6	1	8	2	5

196

5	8	7	3	4	2	9	6	1
4	1	3	9	7	6	8	5	2
6	9	2	5	8	1	7	3	4
1	7	4	2	6	3	5	8	9
2	3	9	7	5	8	1	4	6
8	5	6	1	9	4	2	7	3
7	2	1	4	3	5	6	9	8
3	6	5	8	1	9	4	2	7
9	4	8	6	2	7	3	1	5

197

8	9	2	4	3	6	7	5	1
7	3	6	8	1	5	4	9	2
4	5	1	9	7	2	3	8	6
1	2	3	7	6	8	9	4	5
5	4	9	3	2	1	6	7	8
6	7	8	5	9	4	2	1	3
9	8	5	2	4	3	1	6	7
3	1	7	6	8	9	5	2	4
2	6	4	1	5	7	8	3	9

198

8	9	7	1	3	4	6	5	2
5	3	6	2	7	9	4	1	8
2	4	1	5	6	8	9	7	3
9	7	4	3	5	6	2	8	1
1	5	2	8	4	7	3	9	6
3	6	8	9	1	2	7	4	5
7	8	5	4	2	3	1	6	9
4	1	3	6	9	5	8	2	7
6	2	9	7	8	1	5	3	4

199

5	2	1	7	4	8	3	6	9
7	4	8	6	9	3	1	5	2
3	9	6	1	2	5	4	8	7
2	7	3	5	6	4	9	1	8
9	6	5	8	3	1	7	2	4
1	8	4	2	7	9	6	3	5
6	5	9	3	8	7	2	4	1
8	3	7	4	1	2	5	9	6
4	1	2	9	5	6	8	7	3

200

2	3	4	7	6	8	9	5	1
5	6	7	2	1	9	3	4	8
8	9	1	5	4	3	7	6	2
7	8	5	1	2	4	6	3	9
1	2	9	6	3	5	8	7	4
6	4	3	8	9	7	1	2	5
4	1	6	3	8	2	5	9	7
3	7	2	9	5	1	4	8	6
9	5	8	4	7	6	2	1	3

201

4	1	9	5	3	2	6	8	7
6	8	7	4	9	1	2	5	3
5	3	2	6	8	7	1	9	4
9	2	5	7	6	3	4	1	8
8	7	3	1	4	9	5	6	2
1	4	6	2	5	8	7	3	9
2	9	4	3	1	5	8	7	6
7	5	8	9	2	6	3	4	1
3	6	1	8	7	4	9	2	5

202

4	3	7	9	8	1	2	5	6
8	9	6	2	4	5	3	7	1
5	2	1	7	3	6	4	9	8
9	1	4	6	2	7	8	3	5
3	5	8	1	9	4	6	2	7
7	6	2	8	5	3	1	4	9
6	4	3	5	1	9	7	8	2
2	7	9	3	6	8	5	1	4
1	8	5	4	7	2	9	6	3

203

7	5	6	2	3	8	9	1	4
8	1	2	9	5	4	7	6	3
3	9	4	1	7	6	5	8	2
1	7	5	6	9	3	2	4	8
6	3	8	5	4	2	1	7	9
2	4	9	8	1	7	6	3	5
9	8	1	3	6	5	4	2	7
4	6	3	7	2	9	8	5	1
5	2	7	4	8	1	3	9	6

204

8	4	2	9	1	5	3	6	7
5	9	6	3	7	4	8	1	2
3	1	7	2	8	6	9	5	4
7	2	1	8	4	3	6	9	5
4	6	8	5	9	2	7	3	1
9	3	5	7	6	1	2	4	8
1	7	4	6	2	9	5	8	3
2	5	9	1	3	8	4	7	6
6	8	3	4	5	7	1	2	9

205

7	1	2	9	4	5	8	6	3
8	5	6	3	7	2	1	4	9
4	3	9	6	1	8	2	7	5
2	6	8	5	3	9	4	1	7
3	7	1	2	6	4	5	9	8
5	9	4	1	8	7	6	3	2
9	4	5	7	2	1	3	8	6
1	2	3	8	9	6	7	5	4
6	8	7	4	5	3	9	2	1

206

3	8	6	4	7	9	2	1	5
1	2	4	6	3	5	7	9	8
7	9	5	2	1	8	3	4	6
9	6	7	5	2	1	4	8	3
8	4	2	3	9	6	5	7	1
5	1	3	7	8	4	6	2	9
4	3	9	1	6	7	8	5	2
2	5	1	8	4	3	9	6	7
6	7	8	9	5	2	1	3	4

207

8	3	6	4	2	5	7	9	1
7	2	1	6	9	8	4	3	5
4	5	9	3	1	7	2	6	8
5	1	3	8	7	9	6	4	2
9	7	2	1	4	6	8	5	3
6	8	4	5	3	2	1	7	9
3	6	8	7	5	1	9	2	4
1	9	5	2	6	4	3	8	7
2	4	7	9	8	3	5	1	6

208

7	4	8	5	3	6	1	9	2
2	6	9	8	1	4	5	3	7
3	1	5	2	9	7	6	8	4
4	8	6	1	7	9	2	5	3
5	9	3	6	8	2	4	7	1
1	2	7	3	4	5	9	6	8
8	3	2	9	6	1	7	4	5
9	5	4	7	2	3	8	1	6
6	7	1	4	5	8	3	2	9

209

2	1	3	5	7	9	8	4	6
4	6	9	8	3	2	1	7	5
5	8	7	1	6	4	2	3	9
6	4	8	7	9	3	5	2	1
7	2	5	4	1	8	6	9	3
9	3	1	6	2	5	7	8	4
1	5	2	3	4	7	9	6	8
3	7	6	9	8	1	4	5	2
8	9	4	2	5	6	3	1	7

210

6	3	7	2	1	9	8	4	5
8	1	9	4	5	3	6	7	2
5	4	2	7	6	8	1	9	3
4	9	6	1	2	5	7	3	8
7	2	3	9	8	4	5	1	6
1	8	5	6	3	7	9	2	4
3	6	1	8	9	2	4	5	7
2	7	8	5	4	1	3	6	9
9	5	4	3	7	6	2	8	1

211

5	4	9	2	1	3	8	7	6
8	6	2	7	5	4	3	1	9
1	3	7	8	6	9	5	2	4
3	1	5	9	2	7	4	6	8
2	9	8	4	3	6	1	5	7
4	7	6	1	8	5	9	3	2
9	2	4	5	7	1	6	8	3
6	8	1	3	4	2	7	9	5
7	5	3	6	9	8	2	4	1

212

4	8	6	7	9	2	5	1	3
3	7	9	6	1	5	8	4	2
2	5	1	3	4	8	6	9	7
9	3	5	1	2	6	7	8	4
6	1	2	4	8	7	9	3	5
7	4	8	9	5	3	2	6	1
8	2	3	5	6	4	1	7	9
1	6	4	2	7	9	3	5	8
5	9	7	8	3	1	4	2	6

213

8	6	4	9	2	1	7	5	3
1	3	5	7	4	6	8	2	9
7	9	2	3	5	8	1	6	4
2	1	3	5	6	9	4	7	8
9	8	6	2	7	4	3	1	5
5	4	7	8	1	3	2	9	6
3	7	9	6	8	2	5	4	1
4	2	8	1	9	5	6	3	7
6	5	1	4	3	7	9	8	2

214

7	3	6	8	9	1	5	2	4
9	1	2	6	4	5	8	3	7
8	5	4	2	3	7	6	1	9
3	8	5	7	1	6	9	4	2
4	2	7	9	5	3	1	8	6
6	9	1	4	8	2	3	7	5
1	6	8	5	7	4	2	9	3
2	4	9	3	6	8	7	5	1
5	7	3	1	2	9	4	6	8

215

9	2	3	6	4	8	5	7	1
6	5	8	1	7	3	4	2	9
4	1	7	5	2	9	8	3	6
8	4	1	2	9	6	7	5	3
7	3	6	4	5	1	9	8	2
2	9	5	3	8	7	6	1	4
1	6	4	8	3	5	2	9	7
5	7	2	9	1	4	3	6	8
3	8	9	7	6	2	1	4	5

216

2	8	5	7	4	6	1	3	9
1	6	7	3	9	8	2	5	4
9	4	3	5	2	1	6	8	7
4	5	1	2	8	7	9	6	3
6	7	8	9	1	3	5	4	2
3	9	2	6	5	4	7	1	8
5	1	4	8	7	9	3	2	6
7	2	6	4	3	5	8	9	1
8	3	9	1	6	2	4	7	5

217

7	6	2	3	5	9	1	4	8
8	4	3	6	1	2	9	7	5
9	1	5	4	7	8	2	6	3
5	2	6	1	9	4	8	3	7
1	8	7	5	2	3	6	9	4
4	3	9	7	8	6	5	1	2
6	5	8	9	4	7	3	2	1
3	7	1	2	6	5	4	8	9
2	9	4	8	3	1	7	5	6

218

8	4	1	2	3	9	5	6	7
5	9	2	6	7	1	3	4	8
3	6	7	8	4	5	1	2	9
1	7	3	4	9	2	6	8	5
2	8	4	3	5	6	7	9	1
9	5	6	1	8	7	4	3	2
7	1	8	9	6	3	2	5	4
4	3	5	7	2	8	9	1	6
6	2	9	5	1	4	8	7	3

219

6	1	2	4	9	5	7	3	8
5	3	4	6	8	7	1	2	9
8	9	7	3	1	2	5	6	4
3	4	5	7	6	8	2	9	1
7	2	9	1	5	4	6	8	3
1	8	6	2	3	9	4	7	5
9	5	1	8	7	6	3	4	2
4	6	8	5	2	3	9	1	7
2	7	3	9	4	1	8	5	6

220

7	4	1	2	8	9	6	3	5
5	8	3	6	7	1	4	2	9
2	9	6	3	5	4	8	7	1
1	6	4	9	3	2	5	8	7
8	2	5	4	1	7	3	9	6
9	3	7	8	6	5	2	1	4
4	7	8	5	9	3	1	6	2
6	1	2	7	4	8	9	5	3
3	5	9	1	2	6	7	4	8

221

2	5	6	1	8	4	7	9	3
1	3	7	2	6	9	8	5	4
9	8	4	5	3	7	6	1	2
4	6	8	7	1	3	5	2	9
3	9	5	8	4	2	1	6	7
7	1	2	9	5	6	4	3	8
8	2	1	3	7	5	9	4	6
5	4	9	6	2	8	3	7	1
6	7	3	4	9	1	2	8	5

222

2	3	8	5	6	4	1	9	7
6	5	7	9	3	1	2	4	8
9	1	4	2	8	7	3	5	6
5	9	1	8	2	3	7	6	4
4	8	2	7	9	6	5	3	1
7	6	3	4	1	5	9	8	2
1	2	6	3	5	8	4	7	9
8	4	5	1	7	9	6	2	3
3	7	9	6	4	2	8	1	5

223

4	8	5	7	1	6	9	3	2
6	2	1	9	4	3	8	7	5
3	7	9	5	8	2	1	6	4
1	6	8	4	7	9	5	2	3
7	4	2	1	3	5	6	9	8
5	9	3	6	2	8	4	1	7
9	1	4	3	5	7	2	8	6
2	3	6	8	9	4	7	5	1
8	5	7	2	6	1	3	4	9

224

4	3	7	6	9	5	8	1	2
5	9	2	3	8	1	4	7	6
1	8	6	4	2	7	9	5	3
6	7	8	1	3	9	2	4	5
2	4	9	5	6	8	1	3	7
3	1	5	2	7	4	6	9	8
8	5	3	9	1	2	7	6	4
9	2	4	7	5	6	3	8	1
7	6	1	8	4	3	5	2	9

225

5	1	7	4	3	6	9	2	8
4	3	8	2	9	1	5	6	7
9	6	2	5	8	7	1	4	3
8	2	6	1	4	3	7	5	9
7	9	1	6	5	8	2	3	4
3	5	4	9	7	2	8	1	6
1	8	5	3	6	9	4	7	2
2	7	3	8	1	4	6	9	5
6	4	9	7	2	5	3	8	1

226

9	4	1	3	7	2	6	5	8
2	6	7	8	5	9	1	4	3
8	3	5	1	6	4	2	7	9
7	5	8	4	1	3	9	2	6
6	2	3	7	9	5	4	8	1
4	1	9	6	2	8	7	3	5
1	7	2	5	3	6	8	9	4
3	8	6	9	4	7	5	1	2
5	9	4	2	8	1	3	6	7

227

9	5	2	7	3	8	1	4	6
4	1	3	5	9	6	7	2	8
8	6	7	1	4	2	9	5	3
7	3	5	4	1	9	6	8	2
6	4	8	2	5	7	3	9	1
2	9	1	8	6	3	4	7	5
3	7	6	9	8	5	2	1	4
1	8	9	3	2	4	5	6	7
5	2	4	6	7	1	8	3	9

228

4	9	1	7	3	8	2	6	5
7	8	2	6	4	5	3	1	9
3	5	6	9	1	2	7	4	8
9	2	7	1	5	4	8	3	6
1	6	8	3	7	9	5	2	4
5	3	4	8	2	6	9	7	1
8	1	5	2	6	3	4	9	7
6	4	3	5	9	7	1	8	2
2	7	9	4	8	1	6	5	3

229

8	7	3	6	2	5	4	1	9
9	5	1	4	7	8	2	6	3
2	4	6	1	3	9	5	8	7
4	3	9	7	1	2	6	5	8
1	6	7	5	8	3	9	4	2
5	8	2	9	6	4	3	7	1
3	2	4	8	5	7	1	9	6
6	9	8	3	4	1	7	2	5
7	1	5	2	9	6	8	3	4

230

2	4	7	5	8	1	6	9	3
1	9	3	4	2	6	7	5	8
5	8	6	3	9	7	1	4	2
6	2	4	7	1	8	9	3	5
8	7	1	9	5	3	2	6	4
9	3	5	2	6	4	8	7	1
7	5	9	1	3	2	4	8	6
4	6	2	8	7	5	3	1	9
3	1	8	6	4	9	5	2	7

231

5	6	8	2	4	1	7	3	9
2	7	1	5	9	3	4	6	8
4	9	3	6	8	7	2	1	5
1	5	2	4	6	8	3	9	7
7	8	4	3	2	9	1	5	6
6	3	9	7	1	5	8	2	4
8	2	7	9	3	6	5	4	1
3	1	6	8	5	4	9	7	2
9	4	5	1	7	2	6	8	3

232

8	9	4	7	5	2	1	6	3
3	7	1	8	4	6	9	5	2
2	6	5	3	1	9	4	8	7
6	8	2	9	3	4	7	1	5
5	4	7	1	6	8	2	3	9
1	3	9	2	7	5	8	4	6
9	5	6	4	2	1	3	7	8
7	1	8	5	9	3	6	2	4
4	2	3	6	8	7	5	9	1

233

4	3	2	1	8	7	6	5	9
5	9	1	6	2	3	4	8	7
6	7	8	9	5	4	2	3	1
7	2	3	8	6	9	1	4	5
8	1	6	5	4	2	9	7	3
9	4	5	7	3	1	8	6	2
1	6	4	2	7	5	3	9	8
3	5	9	4	1	8	7	2	6
2	8	7	3	9	6	5	1	4

234

6	9	7	3	2	4	8	1	5
3	8	4	5	1	6	7	9	2
5	2	1	7	9	8	4	6	3
2	6	3	9	8	5	1	7	4
8	7	9	4	3	1	2	5	6
4	1	5	6	7	2	3	8	9
1	5	6	8	4	3	9	2	7
9	4	2	1	5	7	6	3	8
7	3	8	2	6	9	5	4	1

235

7	8	6	2	3	1	5	9	4
2	3	1	4	9	5	6	8	7
4	9	5	7	6	8	3	2	1
6	4	3	5	2	9	7	1	8
9	5	7	1	8	6	2	4	3
1	2	8	3	4	7	9	5	6
3	7	9	8	1	2	4	6	5
8	6	4	9	5	3	1	7	2
5	1	2	6	7	4	8	3	9

236

1	7	6	4	2	9	8	5	3
3	9	8	1	7	5	6	2	4
2	5	4	8	6	3	7	9	1
8	6	1	5	4	2	3	7	9
7	4	9	3	8	6	2	1	5
5	3	2	9	1	7	4	6	8
9	2	3	7	5	8	1	4	6
6	1	5	2	3	4	9	8	7
4	8	7	6	9	1	5	3	2

237

9	5	6	2	1	8	4	7	3
8	7	2	4	3	6	9	1	5
4	3	1	5	9	7	6	8	2
2	1	7	9	8	4	3	5	6
5	4	3	6	7	2	1	9	8
6	9	8	1	5	3	2	4	7
7	6	4	8	2	9	5	3	1
1	8	9	3	6	5	7	2	4
3	2	5	7	4	1	8	6	9

238

4	6	8	2	7	9	3	1	5
9	3	7	8	1	5	2	4	6
2	5	1	6	3	4	9	8	7
5	9	6	3	2	8	1	7	4
1	4	2	9	6	7	5	3	8
7	8	3	4	5	1	6	2	9
8	1	9	5	4	2	7	6	3
3	2	5	7	8	6	4	9	1
6	7	4	1	9	3	8	5	2

239

8	7	1	9	4	5	2	3	6
4	5	3	7	6	2	1	8	9
9	6	2	3	8	1	7	4	5
6	9	4	8	7	3	5	2	1
5	2	7	1	9	4	8	6	3
1	3	8	2	5	6	4	9	7
3	1	9	4	2	7	6	5	8
7	4	6	5	3	8	9	1	2
2	8	5	6	1	9	3	7	4

240

5	2	3	1	4	9	8	6	7
9	8	4	3	6	7	1	2	5
6	1	7	8	5	2	3	4	9
8	4	1	9	2	5	7	3	6
3	9	6	4	7	8	5	1	2
7	5	2	6	1	3	9	8	4
4	7	9	2	3	1	6	5	8
2	3	5	7	8	6	4	9	1
1	6	8	5	9	4	2	7	3

241

6	9	1	4	2	8	5	3	7
4	8	5	3	1	7	6	2	9
7	3	2	9	5	6	4	1	8
8	1	6	5	7	9	2	4	3
2	4	3	6	8	1	9	7	5
9	5	7	2	3	4	1	8	6
5	6	8	1	4	3	7	9	2
3	2	4	7	9	5	8	6	1
1	7	9	8	6	2	3	5	4

242

7	2	6	3	4	1	9	5	8
3	8	4	5	9	2	6	1	7
9	1	5	7	6	8	4	3	2
2	3	9	8	5	6	1	7	4
5	7	1	9	2	4	8	6	3
4	6	8	1	7	3	2	9	5
8	5	2	6	1	7	3	4	9
1	4	7	2	3	9	5	8	6
6	9	3	4	8	5	7	2	1

243

7	5	1	2	8	4	6	9	3
9	6	4	5	1	3	7	8	2
8	3	2	7	9	6	4	5	1
4	8	5	9	3	2	1	6	7
2	7	3	6	5	1	8	4	9
6	1	9	4	7	8	2	3	5
1	4	8	3	2	5	9	7	6
5	2	7	8	6	9	3	1	4
3	9	6	1	4	7	5	2	8

244

8	6	2	4	7	9	5	1	3
7	9	1	6	3	5	2	8	4
3	4	5	1	2	8	9	6	7
4	1	3	9	8	2	6	7	5
9	5	6	3	1	7	4	2	8
2	8	7	5	6	4	3	9	1
5	2	8	7	9	3	1	4	6
1	3	9	8	4	6	7	5	2
6	7	4	2	5	1	8	3	9

245

5	2	8	1	9	7	3	6	4
9	4	3	6	8	5	1	2	7
1	7	6	3	2	4	5	8	9
3	6	7	8	5	1	4	9	2
2	8	9	4	3	6	7	5	1
4	5	1	9	7	2	8	3	6
8	9	2	7	4	3	6	1	5
6	3	4	5	1	9	2	7	8
7	1	5	2	6	8	9	4	3

246

1	2	5	4	9	3	7	6	8
8	6	9	2	7	5	3	1	4
3	4	7	1	8	6	2	9	5
5	3	1	9	6	7	8	4	2
2	9	6	5	4	8	1	3	7
4	7	8	3	1	2	6	5	9
6	1	2	7	5	4	9	8	3
7	8	4	6	3	9	5	2	1
9	5	3	8	2	1	4	7	6

247

6	9	5	8	4	1	7	3	2
8	7	3	2	9	5	4	1	6
4	1	2	7	3	6	5	8	9
5	6	7	9	8	3	2	4	1
9	3	4	1	5	2	8	6	7
2	8	1	4	6	7	3	9	5
3	2	6	5	1	8	9	7	4
7	4	8	6	2	9	1	5	3
1	5	9	3	7	4	6	2	8

248

6	2	3	9	8	5	1	4	7
5	4	9	1	7	3	2	6	8
1	8	7	4	6	2	5	3	9
8	1	2	5	4	9	3	7	6
7	3	5	6	2	8	4	9	1
9	6	4	7	3	1	8	5	2
4	9	8	3	1	6	7	2	5
3	5	1	2	9	7	6	8	4
2	7	6	8	5	4	9	1	3

249

3	5	7	4	6	9	8	2	1
4	1	9	8	2	5	7	6	3
6	8	2	3	1	7	9	4	5
5	6	8	1	9	4	3	7	2
9	3	1	2	7	8	4	5	6
7	2	4	5	3	6	1	8	9
1	9	5	7	8	2	6	3	4
2	7	3	6	4	1	5	9	8
8	4	6	9	5	3	2	1	7

250

2	3	6	5	9	7	1	4	8
5	8	7	6	1	4	9	3	2
1	9	4	3	8	2	6	7	5
3	4	1	7	6	5	8	2	9
9	2	8	4	3	1	7	5	6
6	7	5	8	2	9	3	1	4
7	5	3	9	4	6	2	8	1
8	6	2	1	5	3	4	9	7
4	1	9	2	7	8	5	6	3

251

5	3	6	9	2	7	4	1	8
2	9	7	8	4	1	3	6	5
4	1	8	5	3	6	9	7	2
1	5	9	2	7	3	8	4	6
3	8	2	4	6	9	7	5	1
7	6	4	1	8	5	2	3	9
6	4	5	3	9	8	1	2	7
9	2	1	7	5	4	6	8	3
8	7	3	6	1	2	5	9	4

252

7	1	2	6	3	4	5	9	8
5	4	6	8	9	7	1	2	3
9	8	3	1	2	5	6	4	7
1	5	4	2	8	3	9	7	6
6	7	8	4	5	9	2	3	1
2	3	9	7	1	6	4	8	5
3	6	1	9	4	8	7	5	2
4	2	5	3	7	1	8	6	9
8	9	7	5	6	2	3	1	4

253

6	4	8	7	9	2	3	5	1
1	5	2	8	3	4	6	7	9
9	3	7	6	5	1	8	4	2
3	2	4	5	1	8	9	6	7
5	1	9	2	6	7	4	3	8
8	7	6	9	4	3	2	1	5
2	6	3	1	8	5	7	9	4
4	8	5	3	7	9	1	2	6
7	9	1	4	2	6	5	8	3

254

7	1	4	8	9	6	2	3	5
5	9	2	1	3	7	8	6	4
6	8	3	4	5	2	7	1	9
9	2	8	3	7	5	1	4	6
1	5	7	2	6	4	9	8	3
3	4	6	9	8	1	5	7	2
8	7	9	6	2	3	4	5	1
4	6	5	7	1	9	3	2	8
2	3	1	5	4	8	6	9	7

255

8	5	4	7	3	6	9	1	2
1	6	3	2	9	5	4	7	8
7	2	9	1	4	8	3	5	6
2	3	1	6	8	7	5	4	9
6	8	7	9	5	4	2	3	1
9	4	5	3	2	1	6	8	7
5	7	8	4	6	2	1	9	3
3	1	2	5	7	9	8	6	4
4	9	6	8	1	3	7	2	5

256

3	2	5	9	1	6	8	4	7
8	1	9	2	7	4	5	3	6
6	7	4	8	5	3	1	9	2
2	6	1	7	3	9	4	8	5
5	9	7	4	6	8	2	1	3
4	3	8	1	2	5	7	6	9
9	4	2	3	8	7	6	5	1
7	5	3	6	4	1	9	2	8
1	8	6	5	9	2	3	7	4

257

8	3	5	6	4	2	7	9	1
6	4	1	9	3	7	5	2	8
7	9	2	8	1	5	3	4	6
3	6	4	5	8	9	2	1	7
5	1	7	4	2	3	6	8	9
9	2	8	1	7	6	4	5	3
4	5	9	7	6	8	1	3	2
1	7	3	2	9	4	8	6	5
2	8	6	3	5	1	9	7	4

258

4	7	5	6	1	2	9	8	3
1	6	8	9	3	7	2	5	4
3	2	9	8	5	4	6	7	1
7	1	6	4	2	8	5	3	9
9	5	4	3	6	1	8	2	7
8	3	2	7	9	5	4	1	6
2	4	3	1	8	6	7	9	5
5	9	7	2	4	3	1	6	8
6	8	1	5	7	9	3	4	2

259

2	8	1	6	9	7	3	5	4
9	6	5	4	8	3	1	7	2
3	4	7	2	1	5	8	9	6
8	7	4	1	6	2	9	3	5
5	3	9	8	7	4	6	2	1
6	1	2	3	5	9	4	8	7
1	9	8	7	2	6	5	4	3
7	5	3	9	4	1	2	6	8
4	2	6	5	3	8	7	1	9

260

1	7	3	2	8	6	9	5	4
9	8	4	5	1	7	6	2	3
5	6	2	9	3	4	8	7	1
3	1	9	7	4	8	5	6	2
8	5	7	6	2	1	3	4	9
2	4	6	3	9	5	1	8	7
6	9	8	4	7	3	2	1	5
4	2	5	1	6	9	7	3	8
7	3	1	8	5	2	4	9	6

261

7	1	9	3	2	5	8	6	4
5	6	8	9	4	1	7	3	2
2	3	4	7	6	8	9	1	5
9	2	5	6	7	3	1	4	8
3	8	6	4	1	9	5	2	7
4	7	1	5	8	2	3	9	6
6	9	7	1	5	4	2	8	3
8	5	3	2	9	6	4	7	1
1	4	2	8	3	7	6	5	9

262

1	5	6	8	7	9	2	3	4
4	2	3	5	1	6	8	7	9
8	9	7	2	4	3	6	5	1
5	4	2	1	6	7	9	8	3
9	7	8	4	3	2	5	1	6
6	3	1	9	8	5	4	2	7
2	6	9	3	5	1	7	4	8
3	8	5	7	9	4	1	6	2
7	1	4	6	2	8	3	9	5

263

9	2	4	1	8	7	3	5	6
8	5	3	9	2	6	7	4	1
6	1	7	4	3	5	9	8	2
2	7	5	6	1	4	8	9	3
1	3	9	5	7	8	6	2	4
4	8	6	2	9	3	1	7	5
3	6	8	7	4	2	5	1	9
7	4	1	3	5	9	2	6	8
5	9	2	8	6	1	4	3	7

264

7	5	1	4	8	3	9	2	6
4	9	3	2	1	6	7	5	8
2	6	8	9	5	7	3	1	4
8	1	7	6	2	9	5	4	3
9	3	4	1	7	5	6	8	2
5	2	6	8	3	4	1	9	7
3	8	9	5	6	2	4	7	1
1	7	5	3	4	8	2	6	9
6	4	2	7	9	1	8	3	5

265

4	8	7	1	9	5	3	2	6
3	6	2	8	7	4	5	9	1
1	5	9	2	3	6	4	8	7
2	7	4	9	5	8	6	1	3
5	9	6	3	1	7	2	4	8
8	3	1	4	6	2	9	7	5
9	1	8	5	2	3	7	6	4
6	2	3	7	4	1	8	5	9
7	4	5	6	8	9	1	3	2

266

6	3	8	4	2	9	5	7	1
9	1	2	7	3	5	4	6	8
5	4	7	6	1	8	2	3	9
7	8	3	1	9	4	6	2	5
1	2	6	5	8	3	9	4	7
4	5	9	2	7	6	1	8	3
8	7	4	9	6	1	3	5	2
3	6	1	8	5	2	7	9	4
2	9	5	3	4	7	8	1	6

267

8	3	4	6	5	1	7	9	2
7	6	9	2	8	3	1	4	5
5	2	1	9	7	4	8	3	6
4	9	6	1	3	2	5	8	7
3	8	7	4	6	5	2	1	9
2	1	5	8	9	7	4	6	3
6	4	8	7	2	9	3	5	1
9	5	2	3	1	8	6	7	4
1	7	3	5	4	6	9	2	8

268

8	5	1	6	2	3	7	4	9
9	4	7	8	5	1	2	6	3
6	3	2	9	4	7	8	1	5
5	6	8	4	9	2	1	3	7
7	2	4	3	1	6	9	5	8
1	9	3	5	7	8	6	2	4
4	7	9	2	6	5	3	8	1
2	8	5	1	3	9	4	7	6
3	1	6	7	8	4	5	9	2

269

5	2	3	9	8	4	1	6	7
7	4	8	3	6	1	9	2	5
1	6	9	7	5	2	4	8	3
4	7	2	6	1	3	5	9	8
3	9	6	8	7	5	2	1	4
8	1	5	4	2	9	7	3	6
2	8	4	5	9	6	3	7	1
6	5	1	2	3	7	8	4	9
9	3	7	1	4	8	6	5	2

270

6	5	4	3	9	2	1	8	7
1	7	2	6	8	4	9	5	3
9	3	8	5	1	7	4	6	2
7	4	5	9	6	8	3	2	1
8	2	9	7	3	1	6	4	5
3	1	6	4	2	5	7	9	8
5	6	7	8	4	3	2	1	9
4	8	1	2	7	9	5	3	6
2	9	3	1	5	6	8	7	4

VERY HARD

271

1	6	3	8	7	9	4	2	5
9	4	8	2	1	5	3	7	6
5	7	2	6	3	4	8	1	9
7	5	6	1	8	2	9	3	4
2	3	9	5	4	7	1	6	8
8	1	4	3	9	6	7	5	2
6	8	7	9	5	1	2	4	3
3	2	1	4	6	8	5	9	7
4	9	5	7	2	3	6	8	1

272

8	7	6	1	9	2	4	3	5
1	4	2	5	6	3	9	7	8
9	3	5	7	4	8	6	1	2
4	2	9	3	8	6	1	5	7
5	6	1	9	2	7	8	4	3
3	8	7	4	1	5	2	6	9
2	5	8	6	7	1	3	9	4
6	9	3	2	5	4	7	8	1
7	1	4	8	3	9	5	2	6

273

5	9	1	7	2	8	6	3	4
2	8	4	3	9	6	1	7	5
6	7	3	5	4	1	2	8	9
8	4	6	2	7	5	3	9	1
9	2	7	8	1	3	5	4	6
3	1	5	9	6	4	7	2	8
1	6	8	4	3	7	9	5	2
7	5	2	1	8	9	4	6	3
4	3	9	6	5	2	8	1	7

274

5	1	7	3	6	8	2	4	9
2	4	8	7	9	1	3	5	6
9	3	6	4	2	5	1	7	8
4	6	3	8	7	9	5	2	1
7	2	9	5	1	6	8	3	4
1	8	5	2	4	3	9	6	7
6	5	2	1	8	4	7	9	3
8	7	4	9	3	2	6	1	5
3	9	1	6	5	7	4	8	2

275

8	3	6	4	2	9	5	7	1
9	1	7	8	5	6	2	4	3
4	2	5	7	3	1	6	8	9
2	7	3	9	1	5	8	6	4
5	9	8	2	6	4	1	3	7
6	4	1	3	7	8	9	2	5
7	5	2	1	8	3	4	9	6
3	6	9	5	4	2	7	1	8
1	8	4	6	9	7	3	5	2

276

4	5	6	2	1	8	3	9	7
2	8	1	3	9	7	4	6	5
9	3	7	4	6	5	2	8	1
1	9	8	6	5	4	7	2	3
3	6	4	7	2	1	9	5	8
7	2	5	9	8	3	1	4	6
6	1	3	8	4	9	5	7	2
5	4	2	1	7	6	8	3	9
8	7	9	5	3	2	6	1	4

277

9	2	6	4	8	5	1	3	7
3	7	4	1	6	2	8	5	9
1	8	5	3	7	9	4	2	6
6	9	7	8	5	4	2	1	3
8	1	2	6	9	3	5	7	4
5	4	3	7	2	1	6	9	8
2	6	8	5	3	7	9	4	1
4	3	9	2	1	8	7	6	5
7	5	1	9	4	6	3	8	2

278

1	9	4	7	5	2	6	3	8
3	7	5	9	8	6	2	4	1
8	2	6	4	1	3	5	9	7
5	6	1	2	4	7	9	8	3
7	4	2	8	3	9	1	6	5
9	8	3	5	6	1	4	7	2
6	5	8	3	2	4	7	1	9
4	3	7	1	9	5	8	2	6
2	1	9	6	7	8	3	5	4

279

1	2	6	5	3	7	9	8	4
7	3	8	4	9	6	2	5	1
4	9	5	2	1	8	7	3	6
9	6	7	1	8	3	5	4	2
2	8	3	9	5	4	6	1	7
5	1	4	7	6	2	3	9	8
6	7	1	3	4	9	8	2	5
8	4	9	6	2	5	1	7	3
3	5	2	8	7	1	4	6	9

280

2	3	5	1	7	8	4	6	9
1	6	7	5	9	4	3	2	8
9	8	4	6	3	2	7	5	1
8	1	2	3	4	6	5	9	7
6	4	9	2	5	7	1	8	3
7	5	3	9	8	1	6	4	2
5	2	1	7	6	9	8	3	4
4	7	6	8	2	3	9	1	5
3	9	8	4	1	5	2	7	6

281

6	9	4	1	3	2	5	7	8
3	8	1	5	9	7	2	4	6
5	2	7	8	4	6	1	3	9
8	1	2	3	6	9	4	5	7
7	3	5	2	8	4	6	9	1
9	4	6	7	5	1	3	8	2
2	6	9	4	7	5	8	1	3
4	7	8	6	1	3	9	2	5
1	5	3	9	2	8	7	6	4

282

4	5	6	3	1	7	8	2	9
9	1	3	2	8	4	5	7	6
7	2	8	6	5	9	4	3	1
6	4	7	5	3	2	1	9	8
2	9	5	1	4	8	7	6	3
8	3	1	7	9	6	2	5	4
1	7	2	4	6	3	9	8	5
5	6	9	8	7	1	3	4	2
3	8	4	9	2	5	6	1	7

283

3	9	8	5	2	6	4	7	1
4	7	5	3	8	1	6	9	2
1	2	6	4	9	7	8	3	5
7	8	1	6	3	2	9	5	4
2	3	4	1	5	9	7	8	6
5	6	9	7	4	8	2	1	3
8	1	2	9	6	3	5	4	7
6	5	7	8	1	4	3	2	9
9	4	3	2	7	5	1	6	8

284

6	9	7	8	5	2	1	3	4
4	8	2	9	1	3	7	6	5
3	5	1	7	4	6	2	9	8
9	2	5	1	6	4	8	7	3
1	6	4	3	7	8	5	2	9
8	7	3	5	2	9	6	4	1
7	4	8	6	3	5	9	1	2
5	3	6	2	9	1	4	8	7
2	1	9	4	8	7	3	5	6

285

8	7	9	6	3	4	1	5	2
3	2	6	8	1	5	7	4	9
1	4	5	7	2	9	6	8	3
5	9	8	3	7	6	2	1	4
2	6	4	9	8	1	3	7	5
7	3	1	5	4	2	9	6	8
6	5	2	4	9	7	8	3	1
9	8	7	1	5	3	4	2	6
4	1	3	2	6	8	5	9	7

286

9	4	2	8	5	6	1	3	7
3	6	7	1	4	2	5	9	8
1	8	5	7	9	3	6	4	2
5	9	6	3	7	8	2	1	4
2	7	4	9	1	5	8	6	3
8	1	3	2	6	4	7	5	9
7	5	8	4	3	1	9	2	6
6	3	9	5	2	7	4	8	1
4	2	1	6	8	9	3	7	5

287

3	4	9	2	1	7	8	6	5
1	8	2	6	5	3	4	7	9
7	5	6	4	9	8	2	1	3
2	9	8	1	4	5	6	3	7
5	3	1	8	7	6	9	2	4
6	7	4	3	2	9	5	8	1
9	1	3	5	6	2	7	4	8
4	6	7	9	8	1	3	5	2
8	2	5	7	3	4	1	9	6

288

5	3	4	8	1	7	6	9	2
9	6	1	2	5	4	3	8	7
2	7	8	9	6	3	4	5	1
4	5	9	3	2	8	1	7	6
7	8	6	4	9	1	2	3	5
3	1	2	6	7	5	9	4	8
8	9	7	1	4	2	5	6	3
6	2	5	7	3	9	8	1	4
1	4	3	5	8	6	7	2	9

289

7	9	1	5	6	8	3	2	4
5	6	4	2	3	9	8	7	1
8	2	3	1	4	7	5	6	9
4	7	2	8	1	6	9	5	3
6	1	8	9	5	3	2	4	7
3	5	9	4	7	2	1	8	6
9	4	6	3	8	5	7	1	2
1	3	5	7	2	4	6	9	8
2	8	7	6	9	1	4	3	5

290

4	6	3	8	1	9	5	2	7
1	5	7	6	3	2	4	9	8
2	9	8	5	7	4	1	6	3
8	7	4	2	6	1	9	3	5
9	2	5	4	8	3	6	7	1
6	3	1	7	9	5	2	8	4
5	8	6	9	4	7	3	1	2
3	4	9	1	2	8	7	5	6
7	1	2	3	5	6	8	4	9

291

5	1	7	3	9	8	4	6	2
3	4	9	1	6	2	7	8	5
2	6	8	5	7	4	1	9	3
1	8	5	6	2	3	9	4	7
4	7	2	9	5	1	6	3	8
9	3	6	8	4	7	5	2	1
8	5	4	7	3	6	2	1	9
6	9	3	2	1	5	8	7	4
7	2	1	4	8	9	3	5	6

292

8	4	5	1	3	6	7	2	9
7	2	6	4	9	8	5	3	1
3	1	9	5	7	2	4	6	8
2	7	3	8	6	9	1	4	5
4	6	8	2	1	5	3	9	7
9	5	1	3	4	7	2	8	6
1	9	4	7	8	3	6	5	2
5	8	7	6	2	4	9	1	3
6	3	2	9	5	1	8	7	4

293

1	9	4	7	3	2	6	5	8
7	3	5	8	6	9	2	1	4
2	6	8	4	1	5	7	3	9
9	5	1	6	2	3	4	8	7
3	7	2	5	8	4	9	6	1
8	4	6	9	7	1	5	2	3
4	8	7	3	5	6	1	9	2
5	2	3	1	9	7	8	4	6
6	1	9	2	4	8	3	7	5

294

4	7	3	2	8	6	9	1	5
6	2	5	1	9	3	4	7	8
1	8	9	5	7	4	6	3	2
3	9	6	7	2	8	1	5	4
8	5	7	3	4	1	2	9	6
2	1	4	9	6	5	7	8	3
9	4	1	8	3	2	5	6	7
5	6	8	4	1	7	3	2	9
7	3	2	6	5	9	8	4	1

295

9	5	7	2	1	8	6	4	3
2	8	3	7	4	6	1	9	5
1	4	6	9	5	3	2	8	7
3	2	9	4	8	7	5	1	6
5	1	4	6	3	2	8	7	9
6	7	8	5	9	1	4	3	2
8	9	5	3	6	4	7	2	1
7	3	1	8	2	5	9	6	4
4	6	2	1	7	9	3	5	8

296

3	2	8	4	6	7	1	5	9
6	1	5	8	3	9	7	4	2
4	9	7	2	5	1	8	3	6
9	6	1	5	2	4	3	7	8
7	8	4	1	9	3	6	2	5
2	5	3	7	8	6	4	9	1
1	4	6	9	7	2	5	8	3
8	3	2	6	4	5	9	1	7
5	7	9	3	1	8	2	6	4

297

5	6	1	9	3	7	4	8	2
8	4	9	6	2	5	3	1	7
7	2	3	1	8	4	6	9	5
6	5	8	4	1	2	9	7	3
1	7	2	5	9	3	8	6	4
3	9	4	8	7	6	2	5	1
9	8	7	2	4	1	5	3	6
2	1	5	3	6	9	7	4	8
4	3	6	7	5	8	1	2	9

298

6	2	1	5	8	7	3	9	4
5	7	4	3	9	1	2	6	8
9	3	8	6	4	2	7	1	5
2	9	5	4	7	6	8	3	1
8	1	6	2	3	5	9	4	7
3	4	7	8	1	9	6	5	2
4	6	3	7	5	8	1	2	9
1	8	2	9	6	4	5	7	3
7	5	9	1	2	3	4	8	6

299

2	1	4	6	3	9	8	7	5
9	8	6	7	5	1	2	4	3
7	5	3	2	4	8	6	9	1
8	3	9	4	7	5	1	6	2
4	2	7	1	8	6	5	3	9
1	6	5	3	9	2	4	8	7
6	9	8	5	1	3	7	2	4
5	4	2	9	6	7	3	1	8
3	7	1	8	2	4	9	5	6

300

3	7	5	4	8	6	2	9	1
2	9	1	3	5	7	4	6	8
4	6	8	1	9	2	7	3	5
5	3	6	9	2	8	1	7	4
9	1	7	5	6	4	3	8	2
8	2	4	7	3	1	6	5	9
7	8	2	6	1	5	9	4	3
6	5	9	2	4	3	8	1	7
1	4	3	8	7	9	5	2	6

301

7	2	6	5	9	8	4	1	3
8	1	5	7	3	4	2	6	9
9	3	4	6	2	1	7	5	8
4	9	1	8	6	3	5	2	7
2	6	7	9	4	5	3	8	1
5	8	3	1	7	2	6	9	4
6	7	2	4	8	9	1	3	5
1	4	8	3	5	6	9	7	2
3	5	9	2	1	7	8	4	6

302

2	3	8	1	9	7	6	4	5
4	1	5	6	3	8	9	7	2
7	6	9	2	5	4	8	1	3
1	7	2	9	8	3	4	5	6
5	9	4	7	2	6	3	8	1
6	8	3	5	4	1	7	2	9
3	2	6	4	7	5	1	9	8
8	5	7	3	1	9	2	6	4
9	4	1	8	6	2	5	3	7

303

5	6	3	7	8	4	2	9	1
1	4	2	5	6	9	7	3	8
7	9	8	2	1	3	4	6	5
8	7	1	4	3	5	9	2	6
9	5	4	6	7	2	8	1	3
3	2	6	8	9	1	5	7	4
4	3	9	1	5	7	6	8	2
2	8	7	3	4	6	1	5	9
6	1	5	9	2	8	3	4	7

304

2	9	4	6	5	8	7	1	3
7	5	3	1	9	2	6	4	8
1	8	6	3	7	4	9	5	2
3	7	1	2	6	5	4	8	9
8	6	2	4	1	9	3	7	5
5	4	9	7	8	3	1	2	6
6	3	5	8	4	1	2	9	7
9	1	7	5	2	6	8	3	4
4	2	8	9	3	7	5	6	1

305

3	1	8	6	7	5	4	9	2
4	2	5	9	3	8	7	1	6
9	6	7	4	2	1	3	8	5
2	8	1	3	9	7	5	6	4
6	5	9	1	4	2	8	3	7
7	4	3	5	8	6	1	2	9
1	7	4	8	6	9	2	5	3
5	3	6	2	1	4	9	7	8
8	9	2	7	5	3	6	4	1

306

9	6	4	5	8	3	7	2	1
5	7	1	9	2	6	3	8	4
2	8	3	1	7	4	6	9	5
6	9	2	8	1	5	4	7	3
1	4	8	3	9	7	2	5	6
3	5	7	4	6	2	9	1	8
4	3	9	7	5	1	8	6	2
7	1	6	2	4	8	5	3	9
8	2	5	6	3	9	1	4	7

307

4	3	5	2	8	9	1	7	6
2	6	1	7	3	5	4	9	8
8	7	9	6	1	4	3	5	2
7	1	6	3	5	2	8	4	9
5	4	8	9	6	1	2	3	7
9	2	3	8	4	7	6	1	5
1	5	2	4	7	8	9	6	3
3	9	7	1	2	6	5	8	4
6	8	4	5	9	3	7	2	1

308

8	9	5	2	7	4	6	3	1
6	1	4	5	3	8	9	2	7
3	2	7	1	9	6	4	5	8
4	5	2	6	1	7	8	9	3
1	8	6	3	2	9	5	7	4
7	3	9	8	4	5	2	1	6
2	6	1	4	5	3	7	8	9
9	4	3	7	8	2	1	6	5
5	7	8	9	6	1	3	4	2

309

8	1	2	3	9	5	7	4	6
6	9	7	8	4	1	2	5	3
4	5	3	2	7	6	9	1	8
9	8	4	1	2	3	5	6	7
5	2	1	7	6	8	3	9	4
3	7	6	4	5	9	8	2	1
1	6	5	9	8	7	4	3	2
2	3	8	5	1	4	6	7	9
7	4	9	6	3	2	1	8	5

310

1	6	2	4	9	5	7	8	3
3	9	5	6	8	7	2	4	1
8	7	4	1	2	3	5	6	9
6	2	7	9	3	1	4	5	8
5	8	3	2	4	6	1	9	7
9	4	1	5	7	8	6	3	2
2	5	6	3	1	9	8	7	4
4	3	8	7	5	2	9	1	6
7	1	9	8	6	4	3	2	5

311

6	7	5	3	9	4	1	8	2
1	8	4	7	5	2	3	9	6
3	2	9	1	8	6	7	4	5
7	4	3	2	6	8	5	1	9
5	9	8	4	7	1	6	2	3
2	6	1	9	3	5	8	7	4
9	5	2	8	1	3	4	6	7
8	3	7	6	4	9	2	5	1
4	1	6	5	2	7	9	3	8

312

1	2	9	8	4	5	3	6	7
6	8	7	2	1	3	9	5	4
3	4	5	7	6	9	2	1	8
7	9	3	6	2	8	5	4	1
5	1	8	9	7	4	6	2	3
2	6	4	3	5	1	7	8	9
9	3	1	5	8	6	4	7	2
4	5	2	1	3	7	8	9	6
8	7	6	4	9	2	1	3	5

313

4	9	7	8	2	5	3	1	6
1	8	3	4	7	6	9	5	2
2	6	5	9	1	3	7	8	4
6	4	1	7	5	8	2	9	3
9	7	8	3	4	2	1	6	5
5	3	2	1	6	9	4	7	8
3	1	4	6	8	7	5	2	9
8	2	9	5	3	1	6	4	7
7	5	6	2	9	4	8	3	1

314

9	2	7	6	4	5	8	3	1
6	4	8	1	2	3	7	5	9
3	1	5	9	8	7	2	4	6
5	9	4	2	6	8	3	1	7
1	8	2	7	3	4	6	9	5
7	3	6	5	9	1	4	8	2
4	6	1	8	7	9	5	2	3
8	7	9	3	5	2	1	6	4
2	5	3	4	1	6	9	7	8

315

5	1	8	2	9	7	3	6	4
2	4	3	5	1	6	7	8	9
9	7	6	3	8	4	2	1	5
7	8	4	9	5	1	6	2	3
1	5	2	7	6	3	4	9	8
3	6	9	8	4	2	1	5	7
8	2	7	1	3	5	9	4	6
6	3	5	4	2	9	8	7	1
4	9	1	6	7	8	5	3	2

316

4	5	1	2	6	9	3	7	8
6	9	7	3	4	8	5	2	1
3	8	2	5	1	7	6	9	4
1	4	5	6	3	2	9	8	7
8	3	6	9	7	4	2	1	5
2	7	9	8	5	1	4	3	6
7	1	3	4	2	6	8	5	9
9	2	4	1	8	5	7	6	3
5	6	8	7	9	3	1	4	2

317

8	1	5	3	7	4	9	2	6
4	6	9	1	2	8	7	3	5
2	7	3	6	9	5	8	4	1
3	5	4	2	8	1	6	7	9
9	2	6	7	5	3	1	8	4
1	8	7	4	6	9	3	5	2
5	3	1	9	4	7	2	6	8
7	4	2	8	1	6	5	9	3
6	9	8	5	3	2	4	1	7

318

6	9	8	2	1	5	3	7	4
7	2	1	4	3	6	9	5	8
3	4	5	9	7	8	2	6	1
9	3	2	6	8	7	4	1	5
1	6	4	5	9	2	7	8	3
8	5	7	3	4	1	6	9	2
2	7	9	1	5	3	8	4	6
5	8	3	7	6	4	1	2	9
4	1	6	8	2	9	5	3	7

319

8	9	4	2	5	6	3	1	7
5	2	1	3	9	7	8	6	4
7	6	3	8	1	4	9	2	5
4	7	8	1	2	9	6	5	3
1	3	6	7	8	5	4	9	2
9	5	2	6	4	3	1	7	8
3	8	9	5	7	1	2	4	6
6	4	5	9	3	2	7	8	1
2	1	7	4	6	8	5	3	9

320

2	3	9	7	6	5	1	4	8
4	5	8	3	1	9	7	2	6
6	1	7	4	8	2	3	5	9
8	9	3	1	5	7	4	6	2
7	6	5	2	9	4	8	1	3
1	4	2	8	3	6	5	9	7
9	8	6	5	4	3	2	7	1
5	2	1	9	7	8	6	3	4
3	7	4	6	2	1	9	8	5

SUDOKU 数独

Make Your Own Sudoku

Make Your Own Sudoku

By Hirofumi Fujiwara, master puzzle maker

Now that you've tried your hand at solving puzzles, why not take your mastery to the next level? Why not create your own? Nikoli makes all of its Sudoku puzzles by hand, and for the first time in print, one of Nikoli's premiere Sudoku makers shows how you, too, can join in the pleasure of handcrafting puzzles. Creating handmade puzzles is a delicate and rewarding practice, requiring patience, balance, and focus.

STEP 1: Decide how many cells to leave blank

To start, decide how many cells in your puzzle will be blank and how many will have numbers filled in. In this tutorial, the final puzzle will have numbers in 28 cells (the squares that are shaded), and 53 cells will be blank.

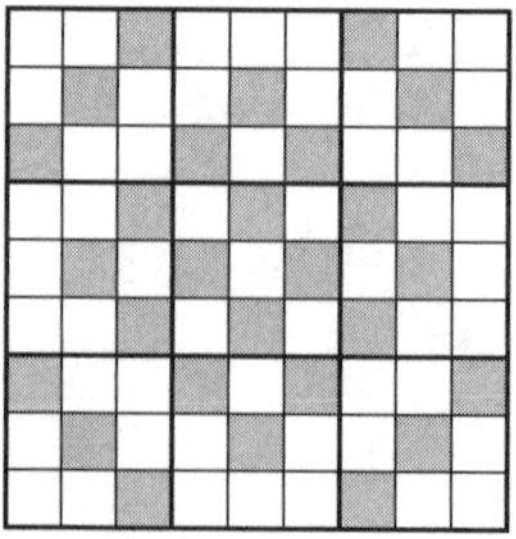

STEP 2: Place the same number in one blank and three shaded cells

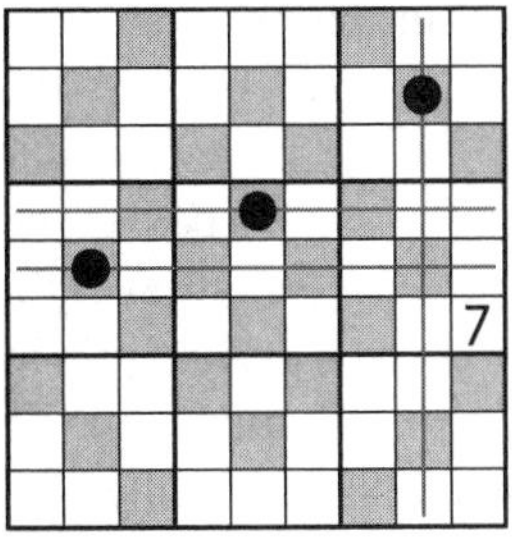

Select a blank cell and place a number in it. In this example, I've put a 7 in the sixth row in the last column. Then, while keeping in mind the original rules of Sudoku (that no number may repeat in any row, column, or 3 x 3 box), I chose one shaded cell from each of the three marked lines and placed a 7 in each (as indicated by the dark circles).

Note: I only placed four 7s because I need to leave as many shaded cells blank for possible use later—if I place too many now, I could end up with an unsolvable puzzle.

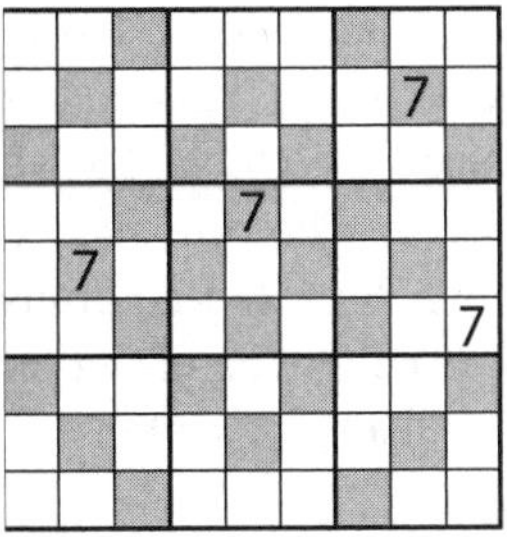

See how the 7s are placed in our example. According to the rules of Sudoku, this fixes 7s in four cells.

STEP 3: Fill in a blank cell that allows you to put the same number in a shaded cell later

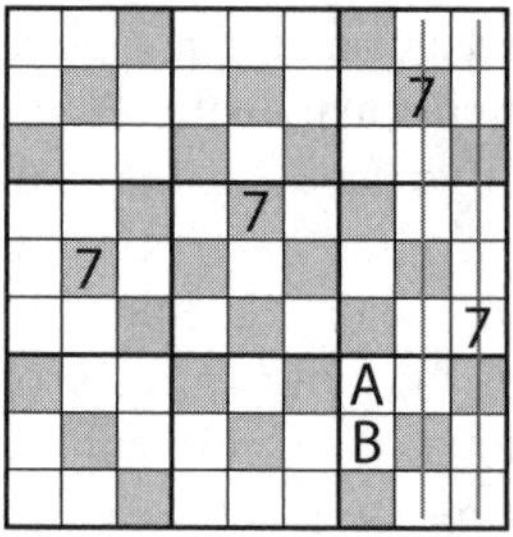

To fill in the rest of the 7s, focus on one box of the puzzle at a time. In our example, a 7 needs to be placed in the bottom right box. There are already 7s in the two columns to the right, marked with lines. Of the three available cells, one is shaded. In this step, we are only placing 7s in blank cells, so a 7 can be put in either cell A or B.

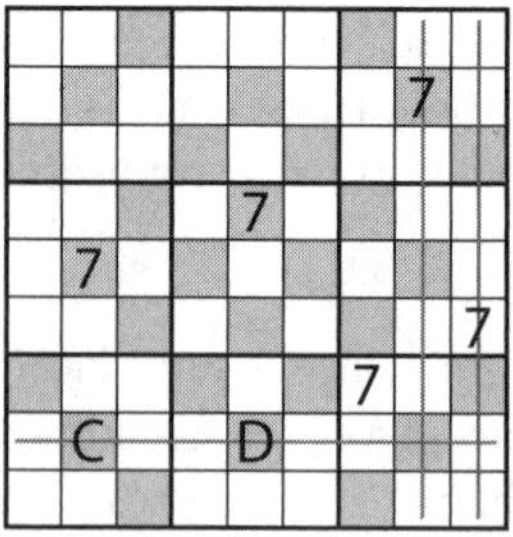

As you can see, I tried putting a 7 in cell A. But in this tutorial, we want to pick a blank cell that will still allow us to put the same number in a shaded cell in adjacent boxes. That means if I place a 7 in cell A, a 7 must be placed in shaded cells C or D. But since there are 7s in the columns above cell C and above cell D, 7s cannot be placed in either of them. Therefore, the 7 must be placed in cell B instead of cell A.

STEP 4: Fill in one shaded cell and two blank ones

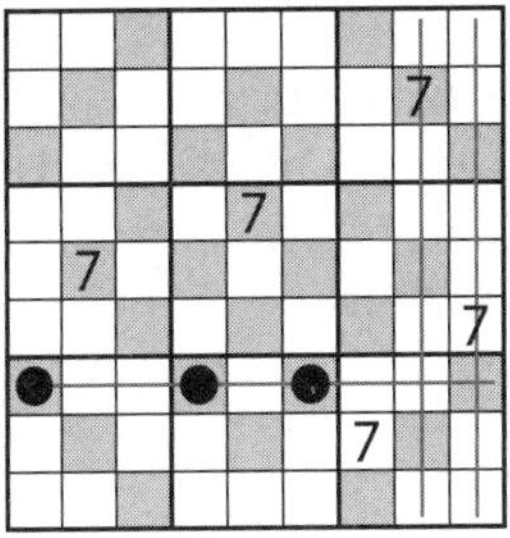

Next, focus on the row above the 7 we just placed. There are three shaded cells along that row that are available (as marked). Try placing a 7 in the middle one.

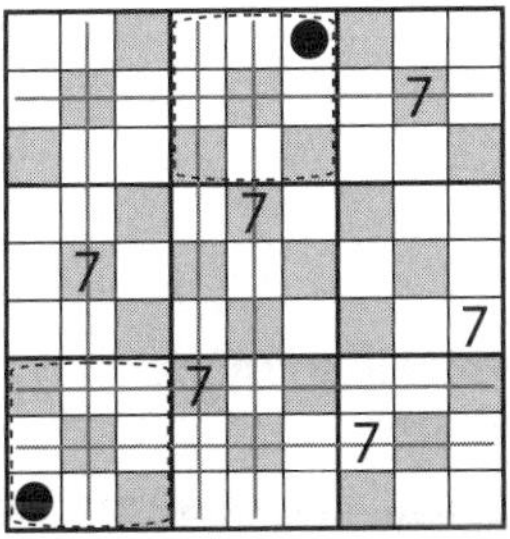

After that 7 is placed, review where our 7s are. A 7 cannot be placed in any cell marked with a line. Now look at the two 3 x 3 boxes (highlighted by dotted lines). No 7s have been placed in either of these two boxes, and both boxes are influenced by three 7s in the columns and rows that intersect them. Avoiding shaded cells, place 7s in each of the blank marked cells.

STEP 5: Put in your ninth number

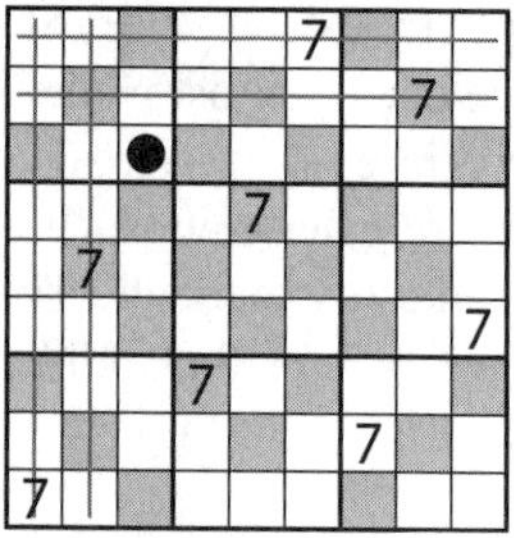

Now that eight 7s have been fixed, there is only one cell available in the remaining box in the top left, as shown.

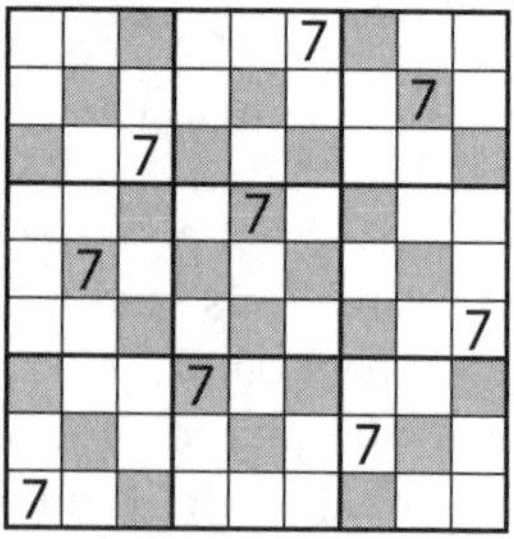

All 7s have now been fixed, with four of them in shaded squares (which will eventually be visible to the puzzle solver).

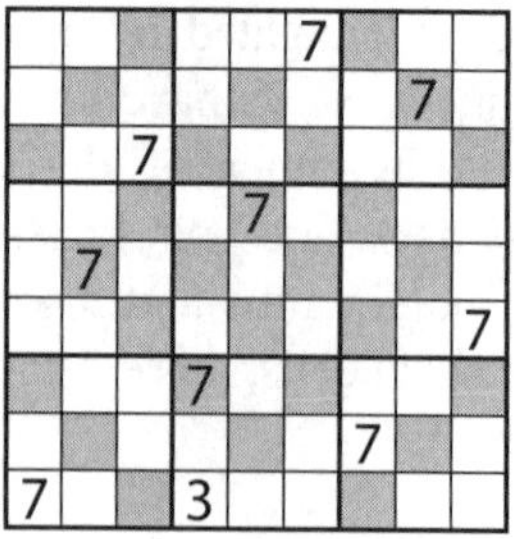

STEP 6: Fill in more numbers

The next step is to fix another number. In this example, I chose 3s to be placed. I set a 3 in an available blank cell, as shown in the grid.

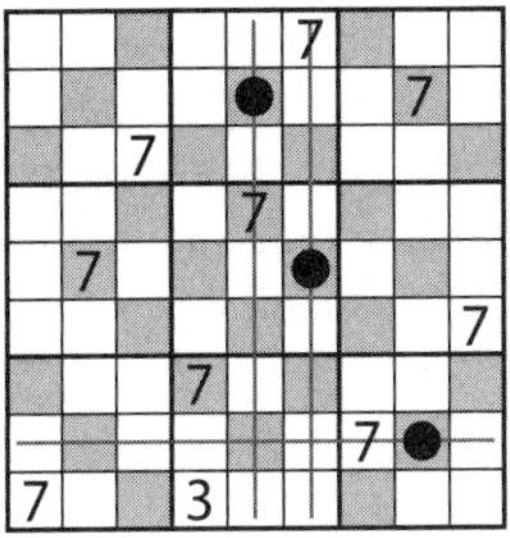

Then, our next task is to fill in three available shaded cells. Based on the placement of our first 3, place a 3 on each of the three lines (outside the box that already contains a 3, of course).

No more 3s should be placed in shaded cells. Therefore, the marked cell becomes 3.

By the same rules, the blank cell marked in the grid also becomes 3.

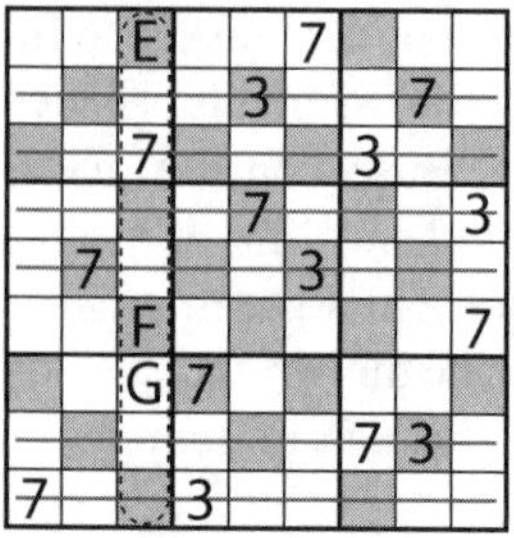

Look at the third column. Since E and F are shaded cells, the only possible cell in which to place a 3 in that column is blank cell G.

We've now fixed seven 3s. There are still two boxes (top left and middle left) with two possible cells in which to place 3s (marked), but they can't be fixed yet.

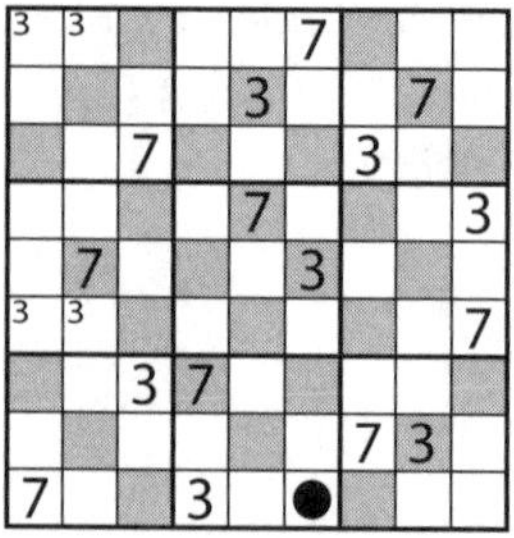

STEP 7: Fill in one blank cell and two shaded ones

I decided to place the 1s next. Try fixing the first 1 in the blank cell indicated in the bottom middle box.

To make that placement work, we have to place 1s in the shaded cells along the lines. In this case, only two shaded cells are available (in the middle box and the bottom left box). Therefore, I am easily able to fix 1s to those shaded cells marked with circles.

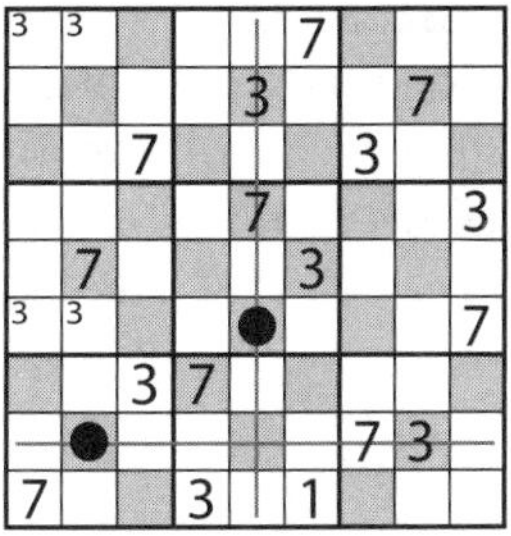

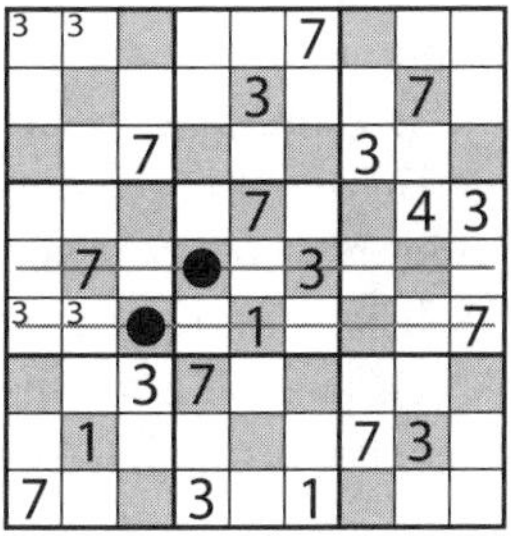

STEP 8: Fill in another blank cell and two shaded ones

Consider other numbers. For example, if I place a 4 in the top center blank cell in the middle right box as shown, I can then place 4s on the marked shaded cells.

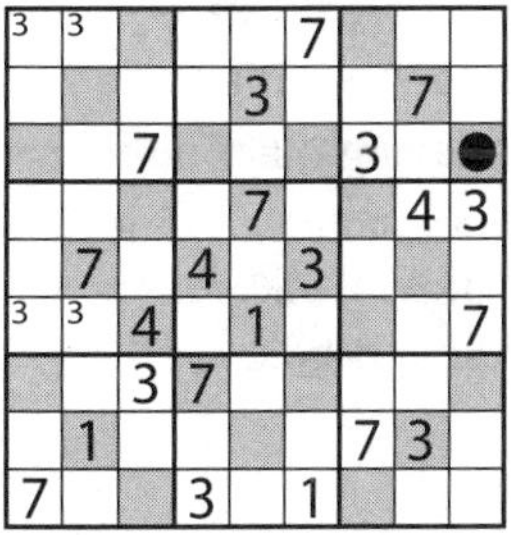

From here, place another 4 in a shaded cell in order to place more 4s in blank cells. Start with the marked cell, for example.

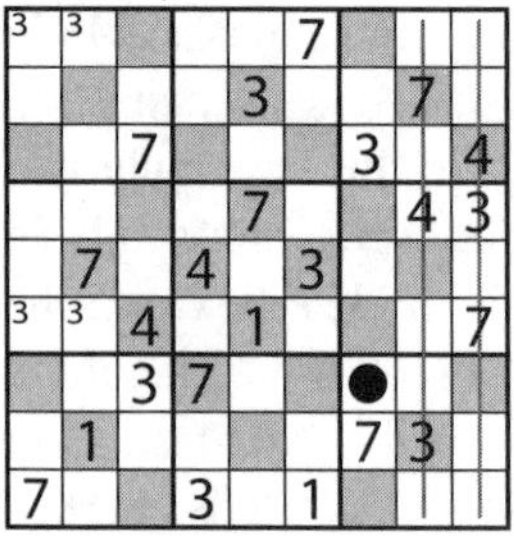

Look at the bottom right box. In that box there is only one possible blank cell in which a 4 can be placed (as marked). Therefore, it will be fixed as a 4.

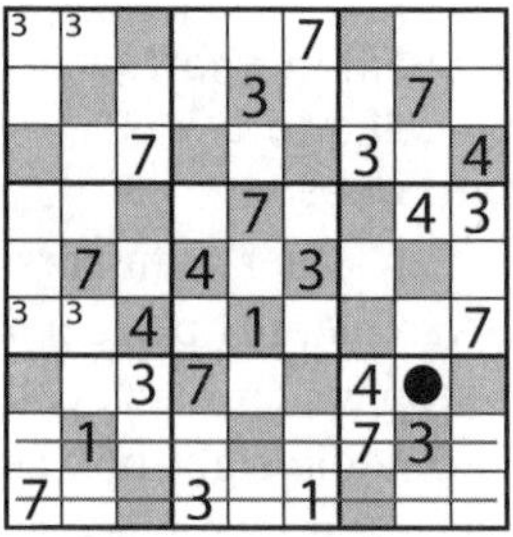

At this point, there are no other possible placements for 4s. But because of the placement of a 4 in the bottom right box, return again to 1s. There is only one blank cell available for the placement of a 1 in that box (marked).

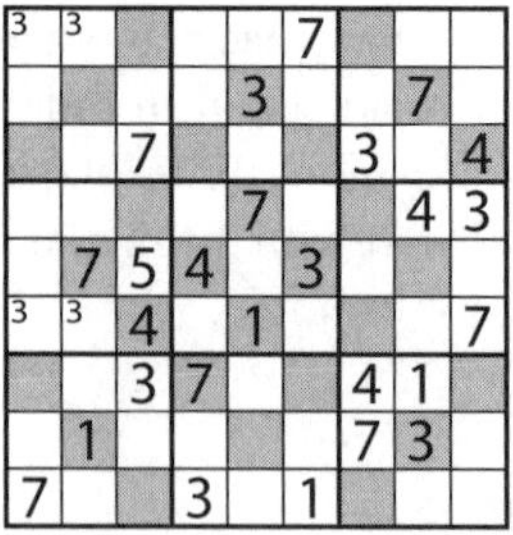

STEP 9: Fix another number to a blank cell

Try placing other numbers. In this example, I've placed a 5 in a blank cell in the middle left box.

If we place 5s on the marked shaded cells along the lines, the 5 placed in the blank cell will be fixed.

Since the 5 in the middle left box is now fixed, a 5 must be placed in the available blank cell (marked) in the middle right box.

It continues, then, that a 5 must be placed in the top right blank cell (marked) as well.

Since two 5s are now fixed in the blank cells in the

top right and middle right boxes, the two marked cells also become 5. Though we are looking to place 5s in blank cells, the only option for placing a 5 in the bottom right box is in a shaded cell, so we place a 5 there.

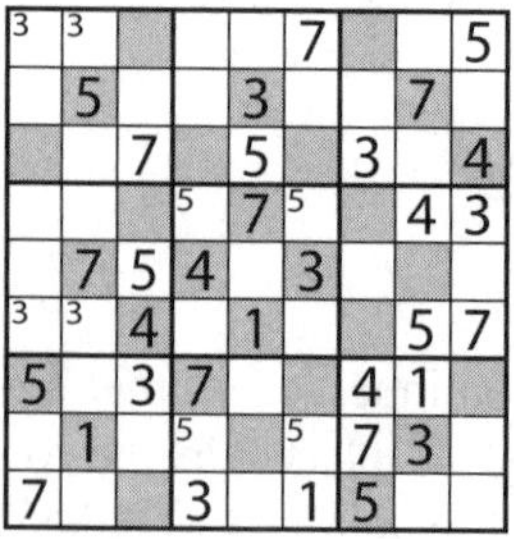

We've now placed seven 5s. Two 5s remain undecided in the bottom two center boxes, as shown.

STEP 10: Fill in one shaded cell and two blank ones

Move on to 6s. In this example, I placed a 6 on the shaded center cell in the bottom center box. Since we

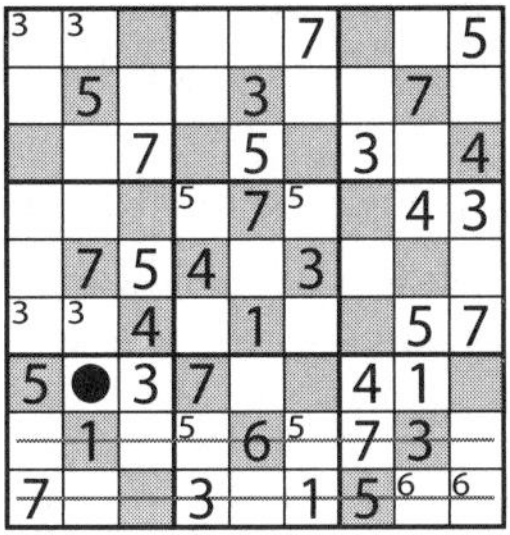

are trying to avoid placing 6s in shaded cells, there is only one available cell in which to place a 6 in the bottom left box (marked). (The two blank cells along the bottom line in the bottom right box are reserved for 6s.)

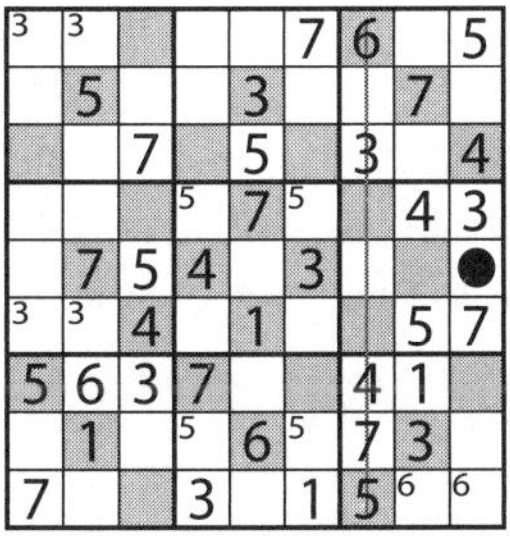

Place a 6 on the shaded cell in the top right box, and we can fix a 6 to the marked blank cell in the middle right box.

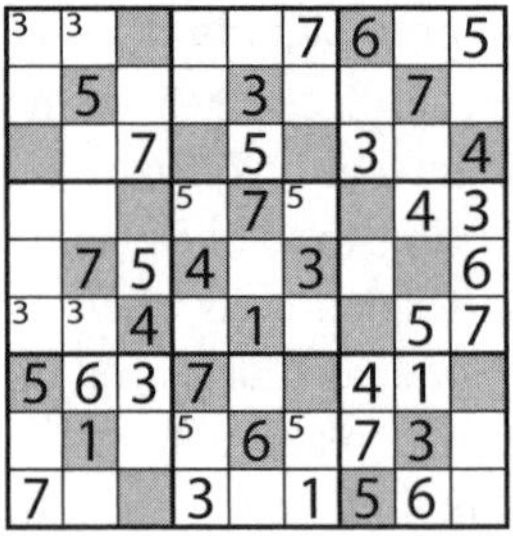

This fixes the 6 in the bottom right box, eliminating one of the two possible placements we marked at the beginning of step 10.

Take a break from 6s, sort out the cells, and check if any other numbers are fixed.

STEP 11: Finishing a number

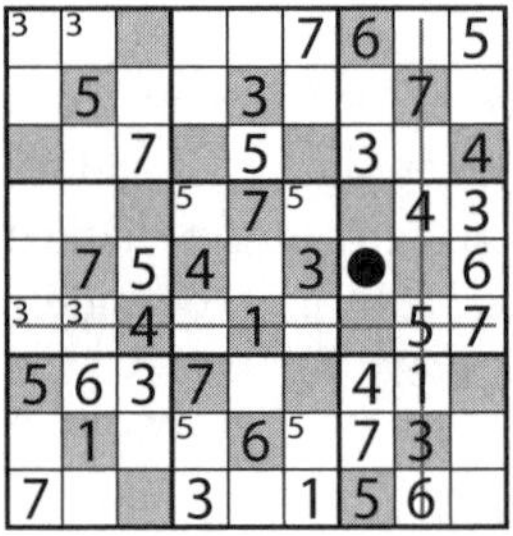

Look at the middle right box. Only one blank cell (marked) is available. With the 1 in the box below, and since we are still trying to limit the number of shaded cells at this stage, the marked cell becomes a 1.

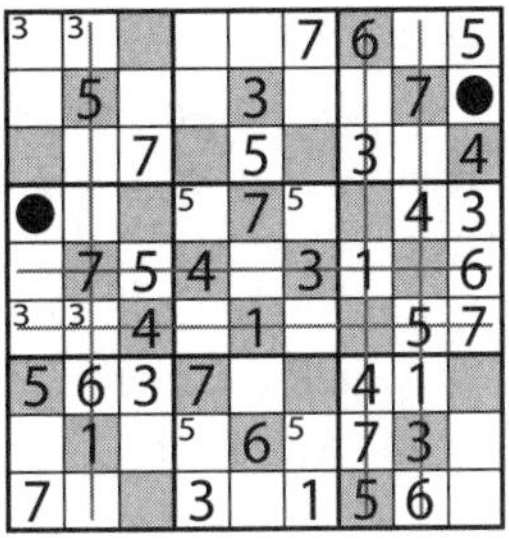

Based on that placement, we can fix two more 1s in the marked blank cells.

Since seven 1s are now fixed, only the placement of two 1s is undecided. Based on the placement of the seven fixed 1s, there are only two possibilities for the two remaining 1s (as marked). They are both shaded cells, but we have no choice.

To review, all nine 1s have now been fixed. We now have both 1s and 7s done.

STEP 12: Consider the constraints of the rows

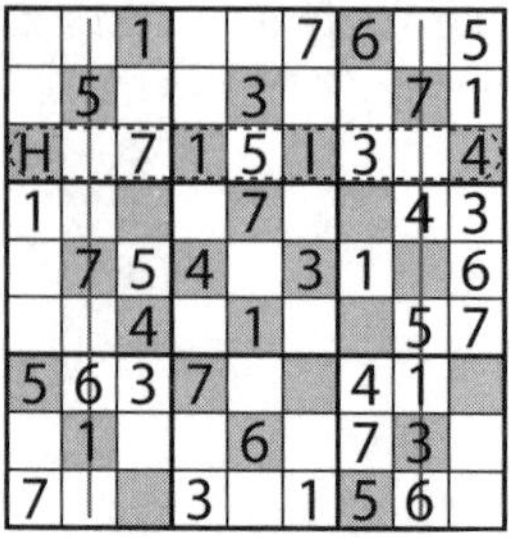

Look at the highlighted row (marked by a dashed line)—it is nearly filled. Note that there are two cells in which a 6 could be placed, marked H and I.

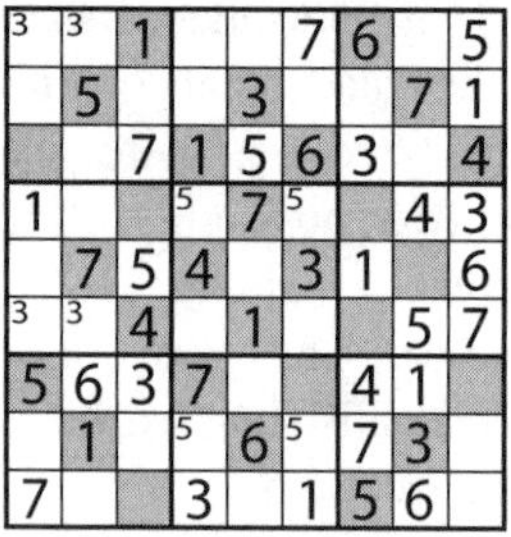

Either placement would work, but for this example, we will choose I. We must proceed carefully once this number has been placed, or the puzzle may break down.

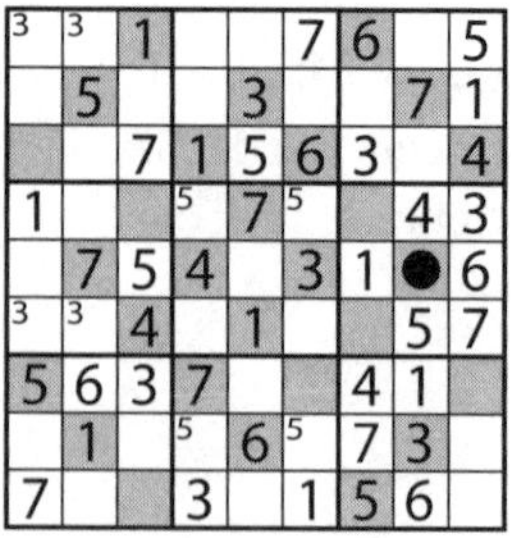

STEP 13: Review the numbers that remain

So far, the unplaced numbers are 2s, 8s, and 9s. In this example, I placed the 9 first, in the marked shaded cell.

Now, using the line as guidance, I placed a 9 in the only available cell in the top right box.

Next, I tried placing a 9 on the shaded cell in the bottom center box (top right cell). Based on that placement, there is only one cell (marked) in the column highlighted by the dashed line that can accept the placement of a 9.

As before, we proceed carefully, so as to avoid reaching an unsolvable puzzle.

Note: At this point, we give up our policy of not placing numbers in the shaded cells.

STEP 14: Fill in remaining numbers

Five 4s have already been placed (see step 8). Look at the highlighted column (indicated by the dashed line). The only possible cell in which to place a 4 in that column is marked. Also, in the top center box, there is only one possible cell in which to place a 4 (marked).

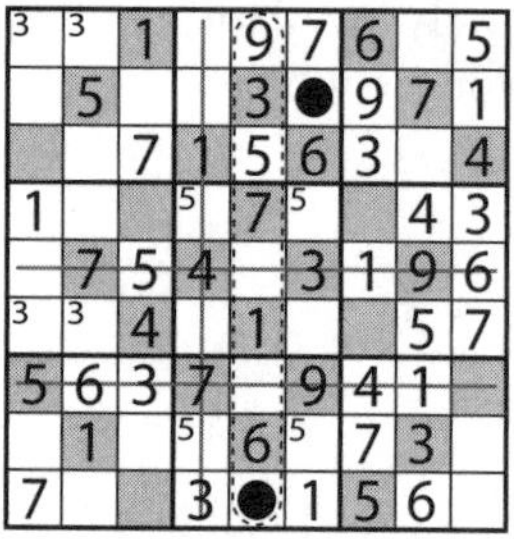

There are only two remaining 4s (that must be placed in both the top left box and the bottom left box). Cell J is the only option for a 4 in the bottom box, and as a result, the remaining 4 gets placed in cell K.

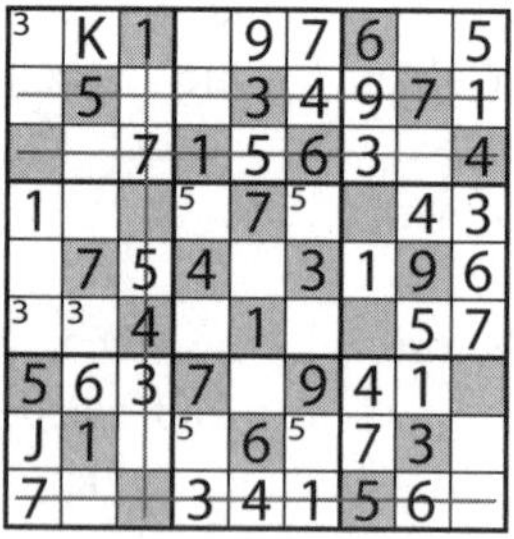

There had been two possible cells in which to place a 3 in the top left box (as first noted at the end of step 6). But now that a 4 has been placed in one of the two cells (cell K), the remaining available cell goes to the 3. To recap, the placement of four number sets has now been completed: 1s, 3s, 4s, and 7s.

3	4	1		9	7	6		5
	5			3	4	9	7	1
		7	1	5	6	3		4
1			^{5}	7	^{5}		4	3
	7	5	4		3	1	9	6
	3	4		1			5	7
5	6	3	7		9	4	1	
4	1		^{5}	6	^{5}	7	3	
7			3	4	1	5	6	

STEP 15. Fill in two more number sets—carefully

3	4	1		9	7	6		5
	5			3	4	9	7	1
		7	1	5	6	3		4
1		M	^{5}	7	^{5}		4	3
	7	5	4	L	3	1	9	6
	3	4		1			5	7
5	6	3	7		9	4	1	
4	1		^{5}	6	^{5}	7	3	
7			3	4	1	5	6	

Look at the middle row of the puzzle, at blank cell L. We can place only a 2 or an 8 in cell L. Let's place a 2 or an 8 on shaded cell M as well, so that cells L and M hold the same number options. If we place the 2s in cells L and M . . .

3	4	1		9	7	6		5
	5			3	4	9	7	1
		7	1	5	6	3		4
1		2	(5)	7	(5)	R	4	3
N	7	5	4	2	3	1	9	6
	3	4		1		Q	5	7
5	6	3	7	O	9	4	1	P
4	1		(5)	6	(5)	7	3	
7			3	4	1	5	6	

. . . then cells N and O become 8s, and cell P becomes 2. Furthermore, a 2 must now be placed in cell Q and an 8 in cell R.

3	4	1		9	7	6		5
	5			3	4	9	7	1
		7	1	5	6	3		4
1		2	(5)	7	(5)	8	4	3
8	7	5	4	2	3	1	9	6
	3	4		1		2	5	7
5	6	3	7	8	9	4	1	2
4	1		(5)	6	(5)	7	3	
7			3	4	1	5	6	

We have now entered more than half of the puzzle's 81 numbers. Check to see if any vacant cells are in fact fixed or not. If this goes unchecked, we risk spoiling the puzzle!

Step 16: Sort out the undecided cells

3	4	1		9	7	6		5
	5			3	4	9	7	1
		7	1	5	6	3		4
1		2	●	7	(5)	8	4	3
8	7	5	4	2	3	1	9	6
	3	4		1		2	5	7
5	6	3	7	8	9	4	1	2
4	1		(5)	6	(5)	7	3	
7			3	4	1	5	6	

Look at the row highlighted by the dashed line and note the locations of 6s in the intersecting columns (marked with lines). The only possible placement of a 6 in that row is in the marked cell.

There had been two possible options for placing a 5 within the center box (see the end of step 9), but now that we've placed a 6 in one of the cell options, the 5 gets placed in the other one. Therefore, a 5 is fixed in the bottom center box, as well.

3	4	1		9	7	6		5
	5			3	4	9	7	1
		7	1	5	6	3		4
1		2	6	7	5	8	4	3
8	7	5	4	2	3	1	9	6
	3	4		1		2	5	7
5	6	3	7	8	9	4	1	2
4	1		5	6		7	3	
7			3	4	1	5	6	

We automatically can fix the numbers 2, 8, 9, 6, and 9 in cells S, T, U, V, and W, respectively.

3	4	1		9	7	6		5
	5			3	4	9	7	1
		7	1	5	6	3		4
1	W	2	6	7	5	8	4	3
8	7	5	4	2	3	1	9	6
V	3	4	U	1	T	2	5	7
5	6	3	7	8	9	4	1	2
4	1		5	6	S	7	3	
7			3	4	1	5	6	

Because of the number 2 in the middle left box, cell X becomes 2, and cell Y becomes 8, the last number in its column.

3	4	1		9	7	6		5
	5			3	4	9	7	1
	Y	7	1	5	6	3		4
1	9	2	6	7	5	8	4	3
8	7	5	4	2	3	1	9	6
6	3	4	9	1	8	2	5	7
5	6	3	7	8	9	4	1	2
4	1		5	6	2	7	3	
7	X		3	4	1	5	6	

3	4	1		9	7	6		5
	5			3	4	9	7	1
●	8	7	1	5	6	3		4
1	9	2	6	7	5	8	4	3
8	7	5	4	2	3	1	9	6
6	3	4	9	1	8	2	5	7
5	6	3	7	8	9	4	1	2
4	1		5	6	2	7	3	
7	2		3	4	1	5	6	

The marked shaded cell is fixed as 9, based on the placement of the 9 in the top right box.

STEP 17: The rest is easy!

3	4	1	c	9	7	6	b	5
e	5	f	d	3	4	9	7	1
9	8	7	1	5	6	3	a	4
1	9	2	6	7	5	8	4	3
8	7	5	4	2	3	1	9	6
6	3	4	9	1	8	2	5	7
5	6	3	7	8	9	4	1	2
4	1		5	6	2	7	3	
7	2		3	4	1	5	6	

Now we place numbers in cells which are the last in their rows, columns, or blocks to be filled in. Cells a, b, c, and d are fixed with the numbers 2, 8, 2, and 8, respectively. Cells e and f are fixed, as well, with the numbers 2 and 6.

We have only four open cells remaining. Those four cells accept 8s or 9s, and there are two ways in which they may be arranged. If all the shaded cells had been used up, two possible answers would have existed, which would have been no good for the puzzle solver. In this example, we luckily do have one shaded cell left.

3	4	1	2	9	7	6	8	5
2	5	6	8	3	4	9	7	1
9	8	7	1	5	6	3	2	4
1	9	2	6	7	5	8	4	3
8	7	5	4	2	3	1	9	6
6	3	4	9	1	8	2	5	7
5	6	3	7	8	9	4	1	2
4	1		5	6	2	7	3	
7	2		3	4	1	5	6	

3	4	1	2	9	7	6	8	5
2	5	6	8	3	4	9	7	1
9	8	7	1	5	6	3	2	4
1	9	2	6	7	5	8	4	3
8	7	5	4	2	3	1	9	6
6	3	4	9	1	8	2	5	7
5	6	3	7	8	9	4	1	2
4	1	9	5	6	2	7	3	8
7	2	8	3	4	1	5	6	9

Place the 8 in that shaded cell (since we already have two 9s in shaded cells), and place the other 8 and two 9s in the remaining cells accordingly.

And we're finished!

STEP 18: Check the puzzle

Once a puzzle has been created, it's important to try solving it. Redraw the actual puzzle, with blank cells hidden. As I solve, I check the following points: Is the way I solve the puzzle as I imagined when I was creating it? Are there any other ways to solve it? Is it fun to solve, or do I want to scrap it?

		1				6		
	5			3			7	
9			1		6			4
		2		7		8		
	7		4		3		9	
		4		1		2		
5			7		9			2
	1			6			3	
		8				5		

STEP 19: Pass the puzzle on

Once we've checked that our puzzle is well-made and solvable, why not pass it to someone else to try? Keep the completed puzzle from the end of step 17 as the solution.

Now that you know how to make Sudoku, make more! It's a good idea for beginners to practice making puzzles that have about 30 shaded cells. Then gradually reduce the number of shaded cells, and when you reach 20 shaded cells (level of difficulty equals "hard"), you'll be ready to apply to be a professional puzzle maker!